The Daily Telegraph
PENSIONS GUIDE

The Daily Telegraph
PENSIONS GUIDE

Barry Stillerman

Stoy Hayward

Acknowledgement

Barry Stillerman would like to express his thanks to Hyman Wolanski BSc (Econ) FIA who, as a consulting actuary, contributed greatly to the material of this book.

Published by Telegraph Publications,
Peterborough Court,
at South Quay,
181 Marsh Wall,
London E14 9SR.

© Telegraph Publications/William Curtis Ltd 1987

This book is sold subject to the condition that it shall not, by way of trade or otherwise, be lent, re-sold, hired out or otherwise circulated without the publisher's prior consent in any form of binding or cover other than that in which it is published.

All rights reserved. No part of this work may be reproduced or transmitted by any means without permission.

Whilst every care has been taken to ensure the accuracy of the contents of this work, no responsibility of loss occasioned to any person acting or refraining from action as a result of any statement in it can be accepted.

Series Editor: Marlene Garsia

Typeset by: Litho Link Ltd., Welshpool

Printed by: Billings & Sons Ltd., Worcester

ISBN 0-86367-224-8 hardback

Contents

Preface	1
Foreword	3
Introduction	5
The winds of change	6
The New Regime	8
Immediate deadlines	9
The political scene	10
The taxation climate	12
Tax-efficiency	13
The changing scene	14
Chapter 1 PENSIONS FOR VALUE	15
What is a pension scheme?	15
Philosophy	18
The problem	19
The cost of retiring	25
The way to proceed	26
Chapter 2 TAX BENEFITS	29
Payment of premiums	30
Inheritance tax planning	34
Chapter 3 TAX-FREE CASH	37
Job mobility	44
Pension mortgages	44

Chapter 4 TIMING YOUR BENEFITS   53
Taking benefits early   53
Taking benefits late   57

Chapter 5 STATE PENSIONS   59
National Insurance contributions   59
The basic retirement pension   61
The State Earnings Related Pension Scheme (SERPS)   61

Chapter 6 GUIDELINES FOR EMPLOYERS   65
Contracting-out   65
The choice of schemes   66
Job mobility   68
The new Personal pension scheme   69
Management of the funds   70

Chapter 7 CONTRACTING-OUT   73
State benefits   74
NIC benefits   75
The '2 per cent' incentive payment   76
The employer's decision   80
The employee's decision   82

Chapter 8 OCCUPATIONAL PENSION SCHEMES   85
Money purchase schemes   86
Final salary schemes   87
The new simplified arrangements   91
Industry-wide schemes   93
Small self-administered schemes   94
Hybrid schemes   96
Executive 'top hat' schemes   96
Loan-backs   98

Chapter 9 ADDITIONAL VOLUNTARY CONTRIBUTIONS 101

Tax benefits	103
Tax-free cash	105
Future contributions	106

Chapter 10 MAXIMUM FUNDING 109

Funding for a pension	110
Widow's pension	118
Life assurance	121
Death-in-service pension	124
Salary sacrifice	124
Over-funding	126
Spreading of relief	127

Chapter 11 JOB MOBILITY 129

Transfers between Occupational schemes	130
Post-1985 service	133
Section 32 policies	134
Personal pension arrangement	135

Chapter 12 SELECTING PERSONAL PENSION SCHEMES 139

Avoiding the pitfalls	140
Pension contributions	143
Minimum contributions and protected rights	148
Benefits	148
Job mobility	151
The pension providers	152

Chapter 13 THE SELF-EMPLOYED APPROACH   153

Personal pension schemes	153
Maximum funding	155
Tax-free cash	156
Inheritance tax	158
Life assurance	159
Doctors and dentists	159
Overseas income	161
Waiver of premiums	162
Self-managed schemes	162

Chapter 14 FOCUS ON INVESTMENT   163

Managed schemes	164
The sector	167
Comparative investments	171
Commission	172
The new players	174
The open-market option	175

Chapter 15 SEEKING IMPARTIAL ADVICE   177

The Financial Services Act 1986	177
Points to consider	178
Impartial advisors	179

Chapter 16 ADMINISTRATION OF PERSONAL PENSION SCHEMES   183

Personal pension scheme certificate	184
Incentive payment for Occupational schemes	185
Other matters	185

APPENDICES 187

Appendix 1	Annuity rates	187
Appendix 2	Income Tax rates 1987/88	188
Appendix 3	Corporation Tax rates 1987/88	189
Appendix 4	Tax treatment of usual forms of investment	190
Appendix 5	Definition of incapacity	191
Appendix 6	Early retirement	192
Appendix 7	National Insurance contribution rates 1987/88	194
Appendix 8	Social security benefits 1987/88	196
Appendix 9	Pension definitions	198
Appendix 10	Pension benefits	200
Appendix 11	Inland Revenue limits — transitional rules	201
Appendix 12	Illustrated funding of a pension scheme — workings	203
Appendix 13	Net relevant earnings	204
Appendix 14	Dependant's pension	206
Appendix 15	Information for an appropriate scheme certificate	207
Appendix 16	Further information on change of circumstances	209

INDEX 211

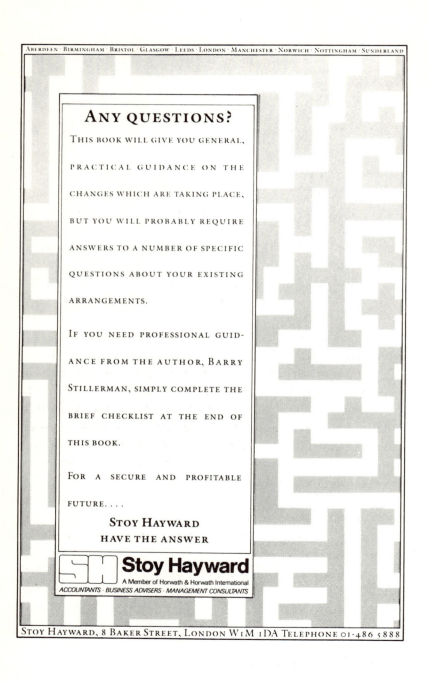

Preface

The changes to the pensions legislation which are outlined in this book will have long-term and far-reaching implications for all employers, the 21 million directors and employees in the UK and the self-employed. These changes have been made following an extensive review, which has been carried out over several years, of the rules and regulations relating to pension schemes and the State benefits. Once the dust has settled and the practical implications of all the changes have been fully absorbed, it is likely that there will be further minor amendments to the law but the Government has indicated that no additional radical changes are planned.

The purpose of this book is to describe the various pension arrangements in general and the new legislation in particular. In view of the short lead-time involved, it is important that you carefully review your own pension scheme, consider the different options which are now available and take professional advice to ensure that appropriate action is taken.

This book is written as a general guide. As any course of action must depend upon your individual circumstances, you are recommended to obtain specific professional advice before you proceed. The Inland Revenue limits are complicated and further advice may be required. Neither *The Daily Telegraph* nor Stoy Hayward can assume legal responsibility for the accuracy of any particular statement in this book.

BARRY STILLERMAN

Foreword

One of the more memorable advertising campaigns of this century is the strip which depicts the man in his twenties who could not care about pensions but who in successive decades, as his cartooned face ages, progresses through considering the subject, to reaching retirement and wishing he had done the right thing earlier.

Possibly it is memorable because it is too near the truth for comfort for most of us. It is not surprising, however, if most younger people have previously glazed-over when the subject of pensions was mentioned for to most employees they are a statutory deduction over which they have no discretion and whose benefit they will not be able to see or assess for decades hence. The deductions are treated merely as involuntary expenditure in the same way as National Insurance or Income Tax. Any investment aspect of the contributions was appreciated only when moving job — and often merely demonstrated what a poor investment it was. Any attempt to understand pensions was likely to become swamped in a jungle of complex regulations which deterred further investigation. The so-called experts on the subject inevitably turned out to be salesmen or agents of the pension policy companies with their own vested interest.

Things are now changing and pensions have moved close to the top of the government's priority list. Having made us a nation of home-owners and share-owners, we are now to be encouraged to invest in our pensions too. There are new laws and regulations and the considerable taxation incentives associated with pensions are being extended to a much wider group of people. Choice has been brought into the equation too. Not only what sort of pension scheme to belong to and which company should manage it — but what benefits are wanted from it and when.

With such choices available to the public it is important to understand pensions better and there is now the financial incentive to do so. A regular valuation of individual holdings in pension schemes should encourage consideration of the contributions as investment rather than expenditure.

Pensions inevitably remain a complex subject — hence this book to guide the reader. The *Daily Telegraph* publishes regular articles on the continuing changes affecting pensions, particularly in its twice weekly Money-go-Round sections, which are the broadest and most comprehensive personal finance sections in any newspaper. However, such articles can neither provide the depth and detail which a book such as this can, nor can they provide the information in such an easily accessible form.

This is a book which can be dipped into occasionally by readers wanting independent clarification of points already mentioned by others in the pensions business, or to answer questions posed by the readers themselves. There are some who may want to read the book cover to cover, but such are the headings of the chapters, that readers should be able to identify immediately whether a particular section will affect them or not. The book is not intended to make readers into experts in the difficult subject of pensions. Its objective is to use the skills of experts to simplify a subject which will be increasingly important to virtually everyone in coming years.

Richard Northedge
Deputy City Editor
Daily Telegraph

Introduction

This book has been written as a practical guide rather than a technical textbook. Its purpose is to explain pension arrangements in general, the significant changes which are now taking place and the options which are open to you. The recent delays to the implementation of these changes indicate the complexity of the task and the necessity to review your arrangements as soon as possible.

While all the chapters should be relevant to employers, employees and the self-employed, for quick reference the following sections may be of particular interest.

The Daily Telegraph Pensions Guide

Chapters	Employers	Employees	Self-employed
Introduction	X	X	X
1 Pensions for Value		X	X
2 Tax Benefits		X	X
3 Tax-free Cash		X	X
4 Timing Your Benefits		X	X
5 State Pensions		X	X
6 Guidelines for Employers	X		
7 Contracting-out	X	X	
8 Occupational Pension Schemes	X	X	
9 Additional Voluntary Contributions	X	X	
10 Maximum Funding	X		
11 Job Mobility	X	X	
12 Selecting Personal Pension Schemes	X	X	X
13 The Self-Employed Approach			X
14 Focus on Investment	X	X	X
15 Seeking Impartial Advice	X	X	X
16 Administration of Personal Pension Schemes	X	X	

The Winds of Change

When Norman Fowler was the Secretary of State for Social Services, he recognised that the country's workforce faced a number of problems. He based his ideas on a review of State and private benefits which had begun in 1983. This review

Introduction

revealed that the current level of national insurance contributions of those in work was unlikely to provide sufficient funds to pay for future State pensions, which in turn would be wholly inadequate in meeting the financial needs of most of those who would receive them. (The number of pensioners is estimated to grow by 42 per cent from 9.3 million in 1985 to 13.2 million by the year 2035. The cost of SERPS is likely to escalate from £200 million in 1985 to £4,000 million by the turn of this century and to £25,000 million by 2033, using November 1985 prices. Meanwhile, the number of contributors is projected to fall by 30 per cent over the next 50 years.)

Only half the workforce (almost 11 million employees) belong to a Company pension scheme, which means that more people should be encouraged to join pension schemes and that existing schemes should be improved so that there is less reliance on the State.

The study confirmed that employees are often unfairly treated when they change jobs, and that social security and pension schemes have been too complex, so discouraging the formation of new arrangements or the introduction of new members into existing schemes. (Over the last 20 years there has been virtually no growth in the number of employees in pension schemes.) The review expressed concern that the pensions industry has become something of a closed shop, with only insurance companies able to run schemes. It also stated that employees who want to improve their pension scheme find it difficult to do so, and those who find themselves in a large scheme do not understand how they will benefit from the fund. Additional considerations are the general trend towards early retirement, and the increase in life expectancy due to medical advances, both of which add to the cost of providing for retirement.

The New Regime

The study of these problems produced much discussion, numerous consultative documents, nearly 4,500 items of written evidence, 7,000 written responses and finally legislation. This included *Improving The Pensions Choice* — an Inland Revenue consultative document published in November 1986. This was followed by *Reforming Social Security* — four sets of draft regulations issued by the DHSS from November 1986, the Social Security Act 1986 and the Finance (No 2) Act 1987.

The Chancellor of the Exchequer, Nigel Lawson, in his Budget speech on 17 March 1987, introduced the new pensions regime as 'a radical transformation in the ways people can provide for their retirement. There are new options for employers and much greater freedom for individuals to plan their own pensions . . .'

The new rules and regulations represent a form of privatisation of pension arrangements and comprise a radical restructuring of the pensions system, offering new opportunities which should not be overlooked. Consequently, this is an ideal time to completely reappraise Individual and Company pension arrangements. Indeed, employers are going to have to review the pension arrangements in the wake of the marketing of the new Personal pension plans and the other changes to the structure of pensions. These changes will affect companies both large and small.

The new regime does not provide an ideal solution. Indeed, there is still a distortion between schemes which were set up under the old rules and those formed under the new legislation. This distortion could act as a stumbling block and make transferring between schemes more difficult unless further action is taken. Other steps which have been taken will have serious long-term effects. Will the tax-free

Introduction

cash limit remain at £150,000 so that it becomes less attractive as inflation erodes its value, or will it be regularly revised upwards?

The changes which are designed to solve some of the above problems are examined in more detail later in this book. These include the privatisation of pensions by contracting out of the State scheme, and the encouragement of individuals to improve their pension entitlement by the introduction of a new Personal pension arrangement in addition to the State scheme. This should provide a greater sense of ownership of pension rights which can now be taken as early as the age of 50. Note, however, that benefits taken at this age will normally be much less than those available at a later age.

The ability for an employee to make a 'one-off' payment into a Company scheme and obtain full tax relief should encourage more pension planning, as will the steps which are designed to make it easier for people to take their pension with them when they change jobs. Other changes include the introduction of a new simplified Company scheme with the minimum of red tape providing 'no frills' benefits and the introduction of banks, building societies and other financial institutions into the pensions arena. The prevention of abuse is tackled by restricting the tax-free cash sum to £150,000 for new schemes and new members of existing schemes, and tightening up the way in which maximum benefits are calculated in Company schemes including the need for 20 (rather than 10) years of service for maximum benefits in some cases.

Immediate Deadlines

While your pension arrangements require a full examination, the following deadlines should be borne in mind.

1. October 1987   From this month employees will be able to make contributions to a 'free-standing' voluntary contribution arrangement outside their Company scheme. The actual date in October had not been determined at the time of going to print. ('One-off' payments are permissible, if the scheme rules permit this, with effect from 7 April 1987.) Employers will need time to set up these arrangements for the employees.

2. 6 April 1988   This is when employees can opt out of their Company's pension scheme without their employer's permission and employers can contract out their money purchase scheme. Any personal pension scheme effected by such employees from 1 July 1988 may be backdated to April 1988 for contracting out purposes.

3. 1 July 1988   The date from which the new Personal pension arrangement can start. The self-employed may wish to maximise their retirement annuity contracts before this date as the method of computing tax-free cash can be more generous than under the new Personal pension scheme arrangements. Employees not in company schemes can take out a Personal pension scheme from 1 July 1988, contract out of the State scheme and qualify for the incentive payment backdated to 1987/88.

The Political Scene

The Government has shown that it favours a form of privatisation of pensions with less reliance upon the State. It has announced that since the cost to the State of providing

Introduction

pensions in the early part of the next century will be an increasing burden there should be a greater emphasis on the individual to make provisions for his own future. The Government announced that no further radical changes are planned to the structure of pension schemes other than those explained in this book. However, since the Government will be in power for not more than five years before calling another election, it is worth noting the present intentions of the other main parties.

The main difference in strategy between the present Government and the Labour Party is that the latter believes the State should meet the cost of the ever-increasing burden to provide for pensions, while the Conservatives want to place the responsibility on the individual.

The Labour Party's manifesto, which was published just before the 1987 election, promised to restore SERPS as part of the process of achieving their objective of a pension level of one-third average earnings for single people and half average earnings for married couples, and to increase existing payments to pensioners. The Labour Party also pledged to repeal the 1986 Social Security Act.

The Alliance's book *The Time Has Come* was also published in the run up to the election, and stated that:

> . . . the reforms to the social security system enacted by the present Government are unjustified and unfair. They will result in a redistribution of income among the poor, a majority of whom will be worse off. The major defects of the system will remain — benefit levels are far too low, some benefits are not taken up and the poor are treated punitively compared with others fortunate enough not to be poor.

The Alliance proposed that 'a long-term pensions policy, including the future of SERPS, must be agreed by all political parties and would promote urgent discussions to achieve that.' It is difficult to see how this could be achieved as the Government would like the burden of SERPS to be 'privatised' and are actively encouraging this by the national insurance savings, while the Labour Party looks to the State to provide these benefits.

The moves toward making pension schemes more flexible and the removal of barriers to job transfer is likely to be an adopted policy of all the parties as a way of producing a fairer system.

The Taxation Climate

The Government has taken steps to make the financial services sector more competitive and to remove anomalies which favour one part of the industry. For example, the removal of life assurance premium relief in 1984 took away a tax advantage of life assurance based investments. It is likely that there will be further changes before this exercise has been completed. (For example, the endowment policy is now less attractive for taxation purposes than a unit trust.) Although it would be logical to remove the tax reliefs which favour pensions over other long-term investments, it is unlikely that the Government would take this step at a time when it is trying to encourage pension planning so as to remove the burden from the State.

Complexity

One of the greatest barriers to pension planning is the complexity of the arrangements and the general lack of awareness of its efficiency as a long-term investment. According to a specially commissioned MORI poll in 1987, 53 per cent of members knew little or nothing about their pension scheme and almost a quarter said that they had never received any information about pensions. One of the objectives of the Government was to produce 'a system that is simpler to understand and better managed'. Clearly there is still a long way to go!

Introduction

Often schemes set up by employers do not receive their deserved gratitude from the staff because they do not appreciate the benefits that they will be receiving. There should be a balance between having sufficient wealth to enjoy yourself during your working life while ensuring that retirement will not become a financial burden, and therefore pension planning should have a role to play for most individuals and their employers.

Tax-efficiency

The tax-efficiency of pensions will be considered in more detail later in the book, but the following simple chart should illustrate the point.

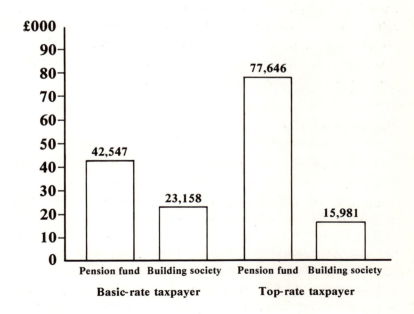

Figure 1.1

The Daily Telegraph Pensions Guide

The Changing Scene

The following are some of the ways in which you could be affected by the changes in the pension rules.

As an employee or self-employed

1. Greater control over your own pension fund.
2. The ability to take pension benefits earlier.
3. It may be easier for you to 'top-up' your scheme.
4. Fewer restrictions on job mobility.
5. A restriction in the use of the tax-free cash sum.
6. National insurance savings by contracting out of SERPS.

As an employer

1. National Insurance savings by contracting out of the State scheme.
2. It may now be easier for you to set up a simple 'easy to understand' pension scheme.
3. More pressure to establish or improve a pension scheme for your staff in the wake of the new Personal pension scheme.
4. Increased job mobility should lead to more mobile staff.
5. Possible changes to the existing scheme due to the new 'free-standing' AVC arrangement.
6. Greater administrative problems in sponsoring the Personal pension schemes.

The implications of the new rules are still subject to change as new regulations are issued and the practical effects of the changes are fully identified. This book is based upon the legislation and regulations which were in force at the end of July 1987.

Chapter 1
Pensions for Value

What is a Pension Scheme?

A pension scheme is a separate fund which is set up by, or for, you to provide benefits on your retirement. It is separately identifiable so that if, for example, a company goes into liquidation, the pension scheme for its directors and employees remains intact.

Money is invested into the pension scheme at regular intervals, normally on a monthly or annual basis. Some schemes are set up by individuals so that only they contribute to their fund, other schemes are completely funded by the employer. However, most schemes will be funded partly by the employer and partly by the employee. In some schemes, Money purchase schemes, the funding level will be one of the main factors which will determine the level of pension benefits whereas in other schemes, Final salary schemes, the benefits provided are those promised under the rules of the scheme. In most pension schemes, the pension fund monies are managed by professional managers, although many schemes allow the money to be invested according to your wishes or those of your employer.

At normal retirement age the scheme must pay the member:

(a) a cash sum; and/or
(b) a pension (ie a regular stream of income) for you and usually your spouse, after your death.

The annual pension is taxable but the cash sum is not. If you elect to take the cash sum, then there will be less in the fund to buy your pension. The pension is an annual payment which will be received for the rest of your life. There are various forms of pension. For example, you could have a Flat-rate pension which will not increase to take account of inflation and will cease when you die, or you could ensure that your beneficiaries continue to receive benefits should you die shortly after retirement by taking a pension which is guaranteed for a term (for example, five years). If death occurs within the five-year period the pension due may be taken as a lump sum. It is also normal to ensure that, after your death, a pension is payable to your spouse. The rate of pension varies depending upon which form you take and also how early you take it. For example, if it runs from age 55 it will produce less than a pension at age 60 which will run for a shorter period.

Once taken, the agreed pension level will not vary, so that if you take a pension which escalates at 7.5 per cent per annum while inflation rises to 10 per cent per annum, the value of the pension will fall in real terms. Annuity rates tend to rise and fall in line with interest rates so that if interest rates seem likely to rise, it may be advisable to defer taking your benefits (if you have a choice) so that you can obtain a better pension. Details of annuity rates as at June 1987 are set out in Appendix 1. These rates are generally lower than those which were available over the past decade and so examples in this book are based upon an annuity rate of 12 per cent.

Perhaps the best way of looking at a pension fund is to think of it as a tank, as illustrated opposite. The direct supply is the pension contributions together with any transfers into the scheme, and the subsidiary supply is the profit made from investing the pension fund money. The pension benefits are drawn from the fund which must be sufficient to ensure that it does not run dry.

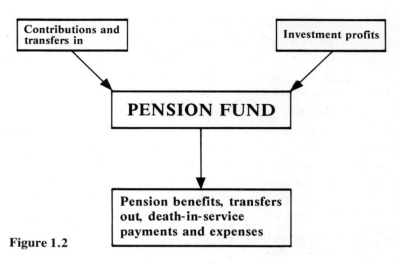

Figure 1.2

The seven stages of life

Table 1.1

Stage	Approximate age	Description
1	Up to mid-teens	Minority — not working — few responsibilities
2	Up to mid-20s	Pre-marriage — working or studying — few responsibilities
3	Up to early 30s	Building a career, marriage and family
4	Up to late 40s	Establishing career — increasing expenditure on home and family
5	Up to mid-50s	Adult children — high earning level — reducing expenditure on home and family
6	Up to mid-60s	Working towards retirement
7	From mid-60s	Retired

This table can only be used as a rough guide and will depend upon factors such as:

(a) whether you were in higher education and went to university;

(b) whether and when you marry and have children;
(c) how early you establish your career and when you hit your peak;
(d) when you wish to retire.

For example, some people would like to retire or semi-retire in their mid-50s whereas others would be unhappy giving up work before they reach their 70s. Some people easily find interests outside their work, while for others work is their main interest.

Philosophy

Your level of pension scheme contributions will normally depend upon the following:

(a) whether you are funding the scheme or your employer is contributing; and
(b) your appreciation of the need and benefits of pension planning; and
(c) your general philosophy; and
(d) your annual outgoings and your ability to save.

You may be the type of person who 'saves for a rainy day' or your attitude may be to 'enjoy today and to hell with tomorrow'. This is all very well but will you be able to live tomorrow at the same standard you enjoy today?

If you are starting a career you may prefer to delay serious consideration of your pension position until your career is established, but you should review the position before changing jobs. You may have very heavy expenditure in the early stages of your career so that you simply cannot afford to fund a pension at maximum level. You may be looking to buy a larger, more expensive house while also meeting school fees so that available money is in short supply. Indeed, if you are looking to 'trade up' your family home, spare cash may be locked up in property for some time. In performance terms, the value of your house may even have beaten your pension scheme over the past five years. However, the tax benefits of pensions and the question mark over whether house prices will continue to rise as sharply in the future show that pension planning should form part of the picture.

Returning to the stages of life (Table 1.1), note that pension planning should be seriously considered by stage 4. It may be too late to provide yourself with an adequate pension if action is delayed until the 20 years or so before retirement. If you take the view that you can make more money by using your entrepreneurial skills during your working life to accumulate capital you will be risking the security of your financial position in your later life. Also the tax benefits of a pension scheme make it more difficult for you to outperform your pension fund and this is considered in more detail later in this book.

The Problem

Over the past decade we have seen a trend towards earlier retirement. In the past it was unusual for a man to retire before 65 years of age. Now retirement at 60 is commonplace and not unusual at 55. The high level of unemployment has become a global problem which is unlikely to be solved in the short term. There is likely to be increasing pressure on successive governments to encourage early retirement or semi-retirement so that more jobs can be taken up in an attempt to reduce the dole queues. Also there is greater emphasis on the quality of life so that people who find that they are able to provide adequately for retirement are looking to retire earlier and engage in other more leisurely pursuits in their later years. The following chart shows that if a man retires at age 65 and a woman at age 60, by far the greatest part of the man's life will have been spent working with relatively little leisure time in retirement. In the case of a woman the post-retirement period is, on average, longer because she retires earlier and lives longer than a man.

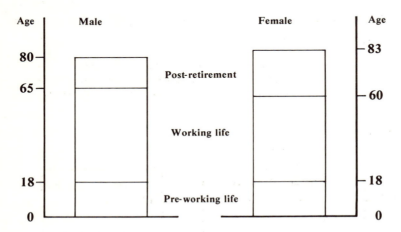

Figure 1.3

Figure 1.3 shows the life expectancy of a man and woman once they have reached retirement age. The life expectancy of an average man may be nearer 75 and that of an average woman may be nearer 80. As mentioned earlier, the other influence in recent years has been the medical advances which have led to an increase in average life expectancy with a consequence of a greater post-retirement age.

With the trend towards earlier retirement you may be nearer to retiring than you think. The new Personal pension arrangements now provide for retirement at age 50. If the trend continues then in another decade the normal retirement age for occupational schemes could also be 50. If you are 40 now, retirement could only be 10 to 15 years away. Unless you are in a good Final salary scheme or a

Pensions for Value

well-funded Money purchase scheme, you may not be able to afford to retire.

The longer you are in a pension scheme, the greater the benefits are likely to be. Also, with regard to Money purchase arrangements, 'the more you (and/or your employer) put in, the more you will get out'. As you will see from the following example, if you do not join a pension scheme until, say, 32, the retirement period would be nearly the same length as your working life.

> An individual started work at 21 and took out a personal pension scheme at 32. He began to maximise the pension scheme contributions from age 40. He retired at 60 and died at 75. His wife died 10 years later.

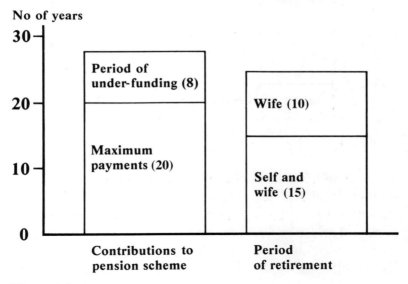

Figure 1.4

You will see from this example that the period of retirement is almost as long as the term during which pension contributions were made so that the resulting pension may be inadequate, especially as maximum contributions were not made throughout the working life.

The expression 'the more you put in, the more you will get out', is further illustrated by the following example.

Table 1.2

A man starts work at 25 on a salary of £7,250. He receives an average increase of 5 per cent per annum and retires at 60 on £40,000. He is in a Money purchase pension scheme from 30 and the fund grows at 10 per cent per annum. The following fund will be produced from the contribution levels as set out below.

Contribution levels	%	%	%
Age 30–39	5.0	7.0	–
Age 40–49	10.0	7.0	10.0
Age 50–59	17.5	7.0	10.0
	£	£	£
Final salary	40,000	40,000	40,000
Value of pension fund	240,000	187,000	135,000
Pension (ignoring tax-free cash) using a 12 per cent annuity rate	29,000	22,000	16,000

The example shown in Table 1.2 is for illustrative purposes only and you will see that the pension from the highest funding rate could exceed the Inland Revenue maximum limit of two-thirds of final salary. It assumes a growth in salary levels of 5 per cent per annum, which is not unreasonable in the current economic climate but is historically low as you may recall the high level of salary increases and inflation during the 1970s. The growth of the fund is 10 per cent per annum. In recent years, due to the bull market in the UK, an annual fund growth of 20 per cent has not been unusual and this is why average contribution levels of 10 to 15 per cent of salary have produced over-funded schemes. However, the stock market has historically been subject to seasonal peaks and troughs and it is unlikely for pension funds to continue to produce such growth if world markets are falling.

Pensions for Value

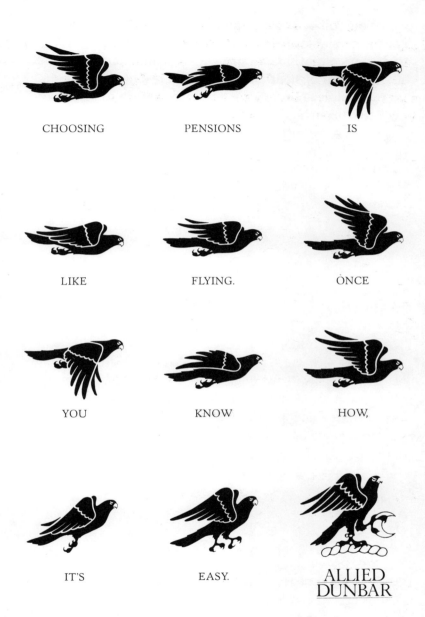

You will see from Table 1.2 that if the total pension contributions start when a person is in his 30s, are increased to 10 per cent of salary during his 40s and increase again to 17.5 per cent of salary in his 50s, the resulting pension may be reasonable. However, if the total contribution is, say, 7 per cent throughout, the pension is unlikely to be adequate. Also it may be insufficient to pay contributions at the rate of, say, 10 per cent per annum from age 40 if no previous payments have been made and contributions at twice that level may be needed to provide a reasonable retirement income under those circumstances.

Inflation

The pensions industry too often produces statistics which show the projected growth of a pension fund and the benefits which will accrue at retirement but take no account of inflation. You should aim to build up a fund which will buy an adequate pension when you retire based on the purchasing power of money at that time after taking account of taxation.

Table 1.3

Married man aged 45 retiring at 60. No tax-free cash is taken.

	£
Projected pension fund at age 60	200,000
Pension from age 60 (at 12 per cent)	24,000
Pension in current terms (discounted at, say, 7.5 per cent)	8,111
Less tax at (say) 27 per cent	(2,190)
Net pension	5,921

Pensions for Value

The example in Table 1.3 has discounted the fund by 7.5 per cent per annum. Although inflation is currently running well below that figure, if you are looking ahead over the next 15 years it would be prudent to assume that inflation will not stay at this low level throughout.

The example in Table 1.3 also assumes a Flat-rate pension of £24,000 per annum at retirement. Those who enjoy Inflation-proof pensions are the fortunate few, and include civil servants, and employees of nationalised industries and local government. If you use your fund to buy a Rising pension to take account of inflation after retirement, the level of pension would initially be less as indicated by the annuity rates in Appendix 1.

The Cost of Retiring

It is difficult to predict accurately how your annual expenditure will be affected after retirement. On the one hand, elderly people have a tendency to spend less on entertainment and travel, and there are unlikely to be any mortgage repayments. On the other hand, there is a greater tendency for elderly people to look after themselves or go into the ever-increasing number of retirement homes, rather than move in with their family. Elderly people are also more likely to require funds for private nursing care. As a rule of thumb, it is estimated that expenditure should fall by one-third in retirement, which is why pensions are often geared towards providing an income stream which is two-thirds of the salary before retirement. It is important, therefore, to consider whether you will be able to maintain an adequate standard of living after retirement, based upon the provisions you have made. Cases have arisen where an individual wishes to retire but cannot afford to do so. This situation must be avoided at all costs.

The Way to Proceed

The entrepreneur may be in the happy position of having accumulated such wealth during his or her lifetime that he does not need to rely upon a pension. He may, for example, have sold his business to produce sufficient cash, after tax, to ensure that he will never be short of money.

Table 1.4

An individual was drawing remuneration of £80,000 per annum as his only source of income and sells his business for £1m.

	£
Proceeds from sale	1,000,000
Capital gains tax after allowances (say)	(250,000)
Net proceeds	750,000
Invested at (say) 12 per cent gross	90,000

Although Table 1.4 shows that the investment income should exceed the salary previously drawn, inflation could result in the income replacement being insufficient in a few years so that capital could be eroded to meet living costs.

Few of us will be in the fortunate position of having accumulated sufficient capital to render a pension unimportant. Those needing to raise extra finance could 'trade down' their home. For example, if you have been living in a four-bedroom house and have seen your children leave home you may no longer need such a large residence. However, people often become so attached to a house that they do not wish to move. Also, the cash which is produced from trading down to, say, a two-bedroom flat does not always produce the large surplus which was originally envisaged.

Table 1.5

	South East £	North West/ West Midlands £	Scotland £
Approx. value of four-bedroom house	120,000	65,000	50,000
Approx. cost of two-bedroom flat	(50,000) 70,000	(25,000) 40,000	(30,000) 20,000
Costs of moving and new furniture	(15,000)	(12,000)	(10,000)
Net proceeds	55,000	28,000	10,000
Investment at (say) 12 per cent gross	6,600	3,360	1,200
Less 27 per cent tax	(1,782)	(907)	(324)
Net increase in income	4,818	2,453	876

As the State pension was not designed to be the sole means of support in retirement, for most people it will be wholly inadequate to meet their ongoing needs. The maximum level of the Flat-rate State pension is currently as follows.

Table 1.6

	Per week £	Per year £
Man from age 65 or woman from 60	39.50	2,054
Married couple	63.25	3,289

Most people will need to reduce expenditure significantly or provide for retirement by ensuring that they have an adequate pension in respect of their earnings during their working life.

It is too often assumed that because you are in a Company pension scheme, your pension will be adequate. You should seek impartial advice from a consultant who can examine your present pension arrangements and then advise you on the level of further contributions which should be made (if any) to 'top-up' your scheme to the required level. If you are an overseas employer, special tax and pensions rules apply and professional advice should be obtained.

Chapter 2
Tax Benefits

Pension schemes have enjoyed special tax benefits since the 1920s. In recent years rumours were circulated that pension schemes may be subject to tax. The very powerful pensions lobby flexed its muscles and no such action was taken. The cynics questioned the motive behind the rumour when it became clear that a substantial volume of pensions business was written before the 1986 Budget.

The need to provide for retirement has been shown earlier in this book. The Government of whichever persuasion will recognise the desirability of avoiding a situation in which the ever-increasing number of elderly people cannot afford to live according to their means. Since the present Government's aim has been to privatise pensions and take away part of the liability of providing for pensions from the State, it is unlikely that the Government will make the job of private pension companies more difficult by restricting tax benefits. This is especially so in view of the volume of the task *which affects 11 million employees in occupational schemes and 10 million who are not*.

Taxation is a very powerful political weapon. Removing tax benefits from pension schemes would be a very unpopular move as it would adversely affect most of the electorate, including higher-rate and basic-rate taxpayers, employers and employees alike. The present Government has pledged that it plans no further significant tax changes in the short-term. Its main target has been to attack the tax-free lump sum rather than the tax-free roll-up sum within pension funds. It is unlikely, but not inconceivable, that the tax status of pension schemes will be disturbed within the next few years. However, if the Government continues with its policy of fiscal equalisation, the tax treatment of pension funds may be reviewed again. In the short-term, the general reduction of income tax rates is likely to have the greatest impact on their comparative tax-efficiency.

Payment of Premiums

The payment into a pension scheme is an allowable deduction for tax purposes. The amount of relief depends upon your income tax position and the top rate of tax you

Table 2.1

An individual is married and pays interest at 12 per cent gross on a mortgage of £30,000 and £1,000 per annum into a pension scheme. Based on the following salary levels, the tax relief would be as follows.

	Person paying income tax at		
	Basic rate of 27 per cent	*Marginal rates of 45 per cent*	*Top rate of 60 per cent*
	£	£	£
Salary	20,000	30,000	50,000
Allowances and charges	(7,395)	(7,395)	(7,395)
Taxable income before pension	12,605	22,605	42,605
Pension payment	1,000	1,000	1,000
Income tax relief	(270)	(450)	(600)
Net cost	730	550	400
Tax relief as a percentage of the net cost of the pension payment	37%	82%	150%

pay. The rates of income tax for 1987/88 are detailed in Appendix 2. The illustration in Table 2.1 compares the tax relief on a pension payment of £1,000 in respect of various levels of income.

You will see from Table 2.1 that the Government will increase your net contribution to the pension scheme by 37 per cent if you are a basic-rate taxpayer and by 150 per cent if you are paying tax at the top rate. If you are an employee and pay under a pension arrangement, basic-rate tax relief will normally be deducted from the payment and any higher-rate relief will be given through the coding notice. If you are self-employed then higher-rate relief will normally be given through your income tax assessment if basic-rate relief is provided under the Personal pension scheme arrangement.

If pension scheme contributions are made partly by the employer and partly by the employee, the employer will also obtain tax relief. If the employer is a partnership or sole trader, relief will be given at income tax rates so that up to 60 per cent relief may be received. If the employer is a company the relief will depend upon the level of profits as

---

Table 2.2

Facts as in Table 2.1. The individual receives a salary of £30,000 but the company contributes 8 per cent and the individual 4 per cent to the pension scheme.

	Company £	Employee £	Total £
Contribution	2,400	1,200	3,600
Tax relief	(840)	(540)	(1,380)
Net cost	1,560	660	2,220
Increase in net cost of pension due to tax relief	54%	82%	62%

set out in Appendix 3, and will be received in the accounting period in which the payment is made.

Tax-free roll-up

Apart from tax relief on contributions made, a pension scheme enjoys a tax-free status so that any income or gains which are made by the fund's investment managers are not taxed. (The only exception to this rule occurs if the scheme managers have been trading, but this situation rarely occurs in practice. However, the Inland Revenue has recently investigated a number of pension funds for trading rather than investing its share portfolios.) The combination of these two factors makes pension schemes one of the most tax-efficient investment vehicles, which is why the Government and the Inland Revenue are constantly on the look-out for areas of abuse.

As most forms of investment suffer income tax at rates of up to 60 per cent and/or capital gains at 30 per cent, the pension fund will normally out-perform a similar personal investment. A summary of investment vehicles which are

Table 2.3

Comparison of the value of a pension fund in which £100,000 is invested for 10 years, with an average investment return of 12 per cent per annum, and a similar investment in a building society deposit account for 10 years, producing a gross return of 12 per cent out of which top rate income tax is paid.

	Pension fund	Building society deposit
	£	£
Investment in year 1	100,000	100,000
Value of investment after year 10	310,584	159,813

Tax Benefits

regularly used is set out in Appendix 4. The benefit from a tax-free roll-up fund can be seen from the example in Table 2.3.

The tax relief on contributions made and the tax-free roll-up is an extremely powerful combination as shown by the following example.

Table 2.4

It is assumed that income at the rate of 12 per cent per annum gross is received and that any tax is paid out of the fund at the end of the year. A comparison of the building society deposit account and a pension fund which rolls up over 10 years is as follows.

	Basic-rate taxpayer		Top-rate taxpayer	
	Pension fund £	Building society £	Pension fund £	Building society £
Net cost	10,000	10,000	10,000	10,000
Add income tax relief	3,699	–	15,000	–
Investment in year one	13,699	10,000	25,000	10,000
Value of fund after 10 years	42,547	23,158	77,646	15,981

Tax deferral

As you will see from Table 2.4, you receive tax relief on the contribution you make to your pension scheme in the year of payment. You are more likely to be able to boost your pension payments during the highest earning period of your working life. This could be the time when your income suffers tax at the higher rates. You may draw your pension upon retirement when the impact of taxation may be less severe. This assumes that your income will be lower in retirement so that your marginal rate of tax will fall. For example, you may pay income tax at the marginal rate of 50 per cent during your working life and become a basic-rate taxpayer paying 27 per cent in retirement.

A lot will also depend, of course, upon the Government's attitude to taxation: the Conservatives are more likely to reduce taxes, while the Labour Party is more likely to increase them. Since 1979, the Government has reduced the top rate of tax on investment income from 98 per cent to 60 per cent and the basic rate from 33 per cent to 27 per cent. It wishes to reduce the basic rate further and it is likely that the rate will be reduced to 25 per cent before long.

Table 2.5

A woman is on an annual salary of £30,000 and makes Personal pension contributions of £1,000 per annum. On retirement a pension of £18,000 per annum will be received.

	£
Pension payment	1,000
Tax relief at 50 per cent	(500)
Net cost	500
Tax relief on pension contribution	50%
Tax payable on pension in retirement	27%

Inheritance Tax Planning

The pension scheme will normally provide for benefits which arise from death while still in employment as a director or employee. On death, the Death-in-service benefits may be paid out of the fund to the trustees who will exercise their discretion as to who should receive the payment. You should sign a letter of wishes indicating who should benefit in the event of your demise. This is not a legally binding document but the trustees normally follow the wishes unless there is a specific reason to ignore them, which would be very unusual in practice. The Death-in-service benefit can be substantial and in Company schemes is normally an amount equal to two or three times final salary plus a pension for the beneficiaries (eg the wife). The benefits payable are dependent upon the rules of the scheme, Inland Revenue limits and the pension scheme having sufficient funds. It may be advisable for the scheme to 'top-up' its funds by insurance where appropriate, to ensure that the maximum benefits can be paid.

If the Death-in-service benefits are paid to the wife, they will form part of her estate and so aggravate the inheritance tax position. However, there is the opportunity to pay the benefits, say, to the children or grandchildren, so that they pass to them without any inheritance tax charge. If the pension is not required to supplement income, it could be advisable to defer taking benefits until age 75 if the

---

Table 2.6

The final remuneration of an individual is £30,000. He dies in service and the pension fund has £120,000 which can be paid to his wife (whose wealth will exceed £330,000 on her death) or children.

	£
Payment to spouse	120,000
Potential inheritance tax at (say) 60 per cent	(72,000)
	48,000
Payment to children without inheritance tax	120,000
Potential tax saving on wife's death	72,000

scheme rules permit, so that the estate can benefit from the potential inheritance tax saving if death occurs before that age.

Chapter 3
Tax-free Cash

One of the most attractive features of a pension scheme is that, on reaching retirement age, part of the accumulated fund can be taken as tax-free cash. However, the commutation of pension for cash reduces the value of the fund so yielding a smaller pension since there will be less money available to provide the pension.

Table 3.1

A man retires at 60 on a salary of £20,000 with an accumulated pension fund of £100,000.

	£
If no tax-free cash taken	
Pension (say) £100,000 at 12 per cent	12,000 per annum
If tax-free cash taken	
Maximum tax-free cash (say)	30,000
Pension (say) £70,000 (£100,000-30,000) at 12 per cent	8,400 per annum

---

For people who were members of a Company pension scheme before 17 March 1987, the maximum tax-free cash which could be taken was a multiple of final remuneration as defined for pension purposes. The level of tax-free cash depends upon length of service. The basic formula for computing tax-free cash is 3/80 for each year of service up to a maximum of 40 years which would attract 120/80 or 150 per cent of final remuneration. However, many employees would not have remained within a scheme for 40 years and the following alternative method of calculating tax-free cash may be used, depending on the rules of the scheme. This is known as the 'uplifted eightieths' scale.

Table 3.2

Years of service to normal retirement date	Maximum allowable tax-free cash as a percentage of final remuneration
Years	% for each year
1–8	3.75
9	37.50
10	45.00
11	52.50
12	60.00
13	67.50
14	78.75
15	90.00
16	101.25
17	112.50
18	123.75
19	135.00
20 or more	150.00

Where this table is used, any cash benefits from previous employments must be taken into account to ensure that the lump sum from all sources does not exceed 150 per cent of final remuneration. The example in Table 3.3 illustrates how the above table can be used to maximise tax-free cash.

The rules in Table 3.2 do not apply to retirement annuity schemes (or the new Personal pension schemes) which are normally taken out by the self-employed (eg a partner in a firm of solicitors). Under the new Personal pension scheme arrangements the maximum lump sum which can be taken is 25 per cent of the total fund when the retirement benefits are taken subject to the limit of £150,000.

Tax-free Cash

Table 3.3

A woman retires on final remuneration of £30,000. She has been in the Company pension scheme for 15 years.

Normal basis	Tax-free cash
£30,000 × 3/80 × 15	£16,875
Uplifted basis	
£30,000 at 90 per cent	£27,000

The abuse

Tax-free cash could be taken as a multiple of final salary therefore it has been possible to fund only for cash. Directors who are also the controlling shareholders of a company may have no outside restrictions as to the salary they draw. The decision may be theirs alone enabling them

Table 3.4

A pension fund of £300,000 has accrued to a controlling director, who has served 20 years with his company and whose annual salary in today's terms has been £60,000. He trebles his salary in three years before retirement and wishes to take the maximum tax-free cash.

Benefits based on final remuneration of £60,000	£
Tax-free cash £60,000 at 150 per cent	90,000
Pension £210,000 at 12 per cent	25,200 per annum

Benefits based on final remuneration of £180,000	
Tax-free cash £180,000 at 150 per cent	270,000
Pension £30,000 at 12 per cent	3,600 per annum

to substantially increase their salary in the three years before retirement so that the final remuneration which forms the basis of calculating tax-free cash is excessive.

The directors who are able to manipulate their salary levels before retirement are able to benefit from additional tax-free cash whereas employees, non-controlling directors and directors of a public company may not be able to do so. Clearly, the opportunity to pay money into a pension fund which is tax deductible, allow the money to roll-up tax-free and then take most of the fund as cash is over-generous, because the purpose behind a pension fund is to produce an income stream in retirement which will replace salary rather than produce tax-free cash.

The changes

If you have been a member of a pension scheme prior to 17 March 1987 then you may still be able to benefit from the above favourable treatment. However, the legislation contains provisions to restrict the entitlement to tax-free cash as follows:

1. The definition of 'final remuneration' will be tightened to avoid artificially inflating this figure, including extending the required employment period (this is considered in more detail in Chapter 10 on Maximum Funding).
2. A limit of £150,000 on the tax-free cash sum, which, in the case of the Personal pension scheme, cannot exceed 25 per cent of the value of the scheme under which the lump sum is paid. The final remuneration, upon which the cash limit is based, is restricted to £100,000. The maximum tax-free cash can only be taken from a Company scheme if the maximum allowable pension is to be received. The right to any payment of the lump sum or pension must not be capable of assignment or surrender.

Tax-free Cash

3. New AVC schemes will no longer be able to be used to fund for tax-free cash. They can only be used to improve the pension benefits.

Special rules have been introduced so that, as mentioned in 2 on the previous page, the level of tax-free cash is dependent upon the level of pension to which the member is entitled.

Table 3.5

A man retires at 65 on a final remuneration of £20,000. He has served 20 years with the company and is in a Final salary pension scheme.

	£
In a 'sixtieths' scheme	
Pension before any tax-free cash £20,000 × 20/60	6,667
Maximum tax-free cash £20,000 × 60/80	15,000
In an 'eightieths' scheme	
Pension before any tax-free cash £20,000 × 20/80	5,000
Maximum tax-free cash £20,000 × 60/80	15,000
In a 'forty-fifths' scheme	
Pension before any tax-free cash £20,000 × 20/45	8,888
Maximum tax-free cash = 'basic rate lump sum and an amount equal to the relevant percentage of the difference between a basic rate lump sum and a maximum rate lump sum'	
ie £15,000 plus $\dfrac{8,888 - 6,667}{13,333 - 6,667} \times (30,000 - 15,000)$	
ie £15,000 plus 33.3 per cent × £15,000	19,995

The illustration in Table 3.5 shows the maximum tax-free cash which can be taken based on three different final salary scheme arrangements.

The relevant percentage as shown in Table 3.5 means 'the difference between a basic rate commutable pension and the employee's full pension expressed as a percentage of the difference between a basic rate commutable pension and a maximum rate commutable pension'.

The restrictions apply to schemes which were set up after 16 March 1987 or to employees and directors who joined existing schemes after that date. It is also understood that the rules as set out on the previous two pages will not apply to schemes which were established before 17 March 1987 but approved by the Inland Revenue after that date. However if a retirement annuity trust scheme, written under Section 226 ICTA 1970, was established before 17 March 1987 and approved by the Inland Revenue but the first contributions were made after that date, then any tax-free lump sum cannot exceed £150,000.

If you have joined your scheme before 17 March 1987 you can still look forward to a tax-free sum of over £150,000 depending upon your level of service and final remuneration but if you now join a scheme then your tax-free cash will be

---

Table 3.6

A woman who has served her company for 20 years retires on final remuneration of £120,000.

	£
Scheme set up before 17 March 1987	
Tax-free cash £120,000 at 150 per cent	180,000
Scheme set up after 16 March 1987	
Tax-free cash £100,000 × 3/80 × 20	75,000

Tax-free Cash

subject to these restrictions. It will be interesting to see whether the ceiling of £150,000 is increased in future years. At present it may seem to be still at a relatively high level as it will only be restrictive if your final remuneration exceeds £100,000 (ie £100,000 at 150 per cent = £150,000).

For schemes set up after 16 March 1987, the tax-free cash limit may be increased to a maximum of £150,000 if the maximum pension is provided. It is quite likely, however, that the ceiling of £150,000 will *not* increase in line with inflation, especially as the Government's philosophy is that the scheme should fund for a pension and not cash. Although not a correct comparison, the mortgage relief limit has certainly not moved up in line with property prices or inflation. It remained at £25,000 for eight years until it was increased to £30,000 with effect from 6 April 1983. If the ceiling of £150,000 is not increased then many employees may find that their tax-free cash is restricted. Inflation and increased earnings levels will result in many senior managers receiving remuneration of more than £100,000 in the future.

Table 3.7

A man is currently receiving a salary of £30,000 per annum and it is assumed that his salary level is likely to increase by 7.5 per cent per annum.

	Man retiring now £	*Man retiring in 20 years* £
Final remuneration	30,000	127,435
Maximum tax-free cash		
— 150 per cent of salary	45,000	191,153
— restricted to	45,000	150,000

Job Mobility

As there are more generous rules for employees who were in a pension scheme before 17 March 1987 there may now be a penalty for employees who change jobs. This penalty is likely to be greater for those who are over 40 and who will not wish to jeopardise their pension rights with less that 20 years to retirement.

If you have been in a pension scheme for some years, by changing jobs now and joining a scheme with a new employer you will be subject to the new rules. This is because even though your employer's scheme may have been running for many years you will become a new member. This may mean that your tax-free lump sum will be smaller than that of your colleagues on the same salary level, as they will have been existing members prior to 17 March 1987. Not only will the different regimes result in penalties for moving jobs but it could make it more difficult to dismiss an executive.

Pension Mortgages

There are three main ways of funding a mortgage to buy a home:

1. A repayment mortgage. This requires you to pay interest on the mortgage and, at the same time, repay the capital of the mortgage. The term is often for 25 years and the payments are normally made at a set monthly level over that period. The payments will increase or decrease only if interest rates change. In the early years most of the payment is interest rather than capital so that the loan is repaid at a quicker rate towards the end of the term.

2. An endowment-linked mortgage. Under this arrangement the mortgage remains constant and you only pay interest and

Tax-free Cash

do not reduce the loan. You also need to take out an endowment policy, which is really a savings plan. The endowment policy should grow in value so that at the end of the mortgage term it matures to pay off the mortgage. A low-cost endowment policy will normally pay off the mortgage and produce a small surplus. A high-cost endowment policy will be more expensive but will produce a greater capital sum.

3. A pension-linked mortgage. If you are in a position to arrange a pension-linked mortgage then you pay only interest on the loan. You also pay money into your pension scheme and use this as your long-term savings plan so that upon retirement, your tax-free cash sum is used to pay off the mortgage. This will require a regular commitment to the pension plan as the tax-free cash projection will normally be computed on the basis of an annual (rather than a single) premium.

Should you die before the mortgage is due to be repaid, the endowment policy and pension arrangement will normally provide sufficient life cover to pay off the loan. Under the repayment mortgage arrangement, separate term assurance may be required. Under the endowment-linked or pension-linked mortgages the investment will need to be well managed to ensure that the projected increase of the fund is achieved. If you follow the pension route you should ensure that after paying off the mortgage, you will have a large enough pension together with any remaining tax-free cash to meet your needs. If so, it will probably be the best and the cheapest way to fund your mortgage.

The repayment mortgage route will require you to pay off the loan by using money which will normally have been saved from your earnings and investment income. As this income will have suffered income tax you will be paying off your mortgage from after-taxed income. The endowment policy suffers from the same problem as the premium of the endowment policy will normally be paid out of the taxed income.

Before March 1984 the endowment policy was an attractive savings vehicle as the premium attracted 15 per cent life assurance relief. This relief is no longer available but it continues for pre-1984 policies so that it may be advisable to retain rather than encash them. As a savings vehicle, the endowment policy is less tax-efficient that the pension plan for two main reasons.

1. The pension fund grows tax-free while corporation tax is levied upon gains made by life companies so that the endowment policy will effectively incur this charge.
2. The premiums paid into a pension plan attract income tax relief at your top marginal rate, while premiums paid to an endowment policy attract no tax relief at all unless it was taken out before 1984. If this is the case the 15 per cent life assurance premium relief will still be received.

The effect of tax relief for pension arrangements can be illustrated from the following statistics which compare the performance of a single premium of £1,000 into a pension

---

Table 3.8

Average performance of a £1,000 lump sum investment over five years on an offer-to-bid basis including net income reinvested.

Sector	Pension fund £	Insurance bond £
UK Equity	3,550	2,824
International	3,063	2,410
North American	2,275	1,880

(*Source: Money Management*, June 1987)

policy, with a similar single premium into a life assurance single premium bond. The above statistics take no account of the tax relief receivable on the pension premium.

These tax breaks make the pension-linked mortgage the cheapest way to finance a house purchase as the following illustration shows.

Table 3.9

A 35-year-old man who is a 60 per cent taxpayer takes out a £30,000 mortgage for a 25 year term. The interest rate is 11 per cent per annum.

Monthly payments	*Repayment mortgage*	*Endowment-linked mortgage*	*Pension-linked mortgage*
	Net	Net	Net
	£	£	£
To lender	166.87	110.00	110.00
Endowment/ pension premium	n/a	41.37	30.76
Life assurance premium (net)	3.52	n/a	3.72
Total payments	170.39	151.37	144.48
Proceeds after repayment of mortgage at end of term	Nil	£16,863	Cash of £7,504 plus pension of £11,481 per annum.

In the past, pension-linked mortgages have not generally been available to employees in Occupational schemes. This is because although the employee would be entitled to tax-free cash upon retirement, it came from a scheme which was not under his control. AVC arrangements have been used to fund a mortgage as previous arrangements were able to produce tax-free cash. Finance houses have been happier to arrange a pension-linked mortgage for controlling directors and employees with individual pension arrangements, ie executive pension plans. Normally the finance house would receive a commitment to pay money into a pension scheme which they would manage and this would produce the tax-free cash to pay off the interest-only loan. The self-employed have found it much easier to arrange this form of mortgage due to the tax-free cash from their retirement annuity.

The restriction in the level of tax-free cash is unlikely to be a major stumbling block to pension mortgages at the present time as most mortgages are below £150,000. At first, the announcement that AVCs will no longer be able to produce tax-free cash pointed to the end of the pension-linked mortgage for employees of Occupational schemes. This would result in a loss of important business for the financial services industry. Several companies now take the view that so long as there is reasonable equity in the property ensuring that the loan is well secured and the tax-free cash from the Company scheme is projected to exceed the loan, this form of mortgage can still be arranged. Therefore employees who are members of Company schemes (whether in an AVC arrangement or not) are likely to find more companies which are willing to offer interest-only, pension-linked mortgages. Indeed, some finance houses are likely to promote the AVC mortgage even though the AVC itself will not produce the tax-free cash!

In an attempt to defend the Occupational scheme against the marketing of the new Personal pension arrangement, many companies may need to make a pension mortgage facility available to their staff. If not, the offer of a mortgage arrangement from a PPS may prove to be too tempting for certain employees.

Tax-free Cash

The controlling directors and executives should be able to arrange pension-linked mortgages as before although, of course, the limit may be reduced. The self-employed can also continue to fund for cash through the retirement annuities and the PPS, although as explained later in the book, the tax-free cash could be greater under the existing retirement annuity arrangement so that urgent action may be required this year to benefit from the existing rules.

Whether there is a growth of pension-linked mortgages on the back of the tax-free cash from a Company scheme remains to be seen. The restriction on benefits due to job transfers could be a problem and this is now receiving a lot of attention. In the current economic climate, interest-only loans are more commonplace. If interest rates were to rise and if the economic growth in the UK slows down there could be a reluctance to lend on this basis.

Table 3.10

A company purchases an office for £200,000 by extending bank borrowings. It pays corporation tax at the rate of 35 per cent and sells the property five years later for £400,000 without reinvesting the proceeds.

	£
Interest payable on £200,000 at (say) 12 per cent	24,000
Corporation tax relief at 35 per cent	(8,400)
Net interest payable	15,600 per annum
Sale of property	400,000
CGT (say)	(50,000)
Net proceeds	350,000

Further tax may be payable when the net proceeds are extracted from the company.

49

As the tax-free cash from a pension scheme can be substantial it can be used to fund the purchase of a very expensive home or the family trading company's office. If a director wishes to buy an office for, say, £200,000 and believes that it will be a very good investment he often has three choices regarding the purchase of the property.

1. *The company*

The company is probably the most logical purchaser and can use the asset for future expansion. However, when it is sold, corporation tax may be payable on the gain (subject to indexation allowance and roll-over relief) and the after-tax proceeds will be locked in the company. Further tax may be payable if the net cash is to be extracted.

2. *The pension fund*

Often small self-administered pension schemes are used to

Table 3.11

The company needs a new office costing £200,000 but it is experiencing financial problems. The pension fund has cash funds of £160,000 and borrows £40,000 to buy the office. It then grants a lease to the company.

Pension fund	£
Rental income from company (say)	16,000
Interest payable on £40,000 at (say) 12 per cent	(4,800)
Tax-free income	11,200
Company	
Payment of rent to pension fund	16,000
Tax relief at (say) 35 per cent	(5,600)
Net cost	10,400

acquire the company premises. Upon its sale no tax would be payable but the benefits could not be unlocked until retirement and only part may be in the form of cash. Also, if in the case of a small scheme, the director is less than 10 years from normal retirement date, the Superannuation Funds Office (SFO) of the Inland Revenue are unlikely to approve the purchase as the property will need to be sold shortly to provide the benefits. If loan finance is required this may be restricted to three times the annual contribution. The commercial rent payable by the company will attract corporation tax relief and will be received tax-free by the pension fund. *(See Table 3.11)*

3. *The director*

If the loan could be financed by way of the future tax-free cash entitlement which is due to the director, then only interest will be paid and this could be partly financed by the rent. Any gain from the sale of the property will be subject

---

Table 3.12

A director wishes to buy the freehold of the company's premises for £200,000 and lease it to the company. An interest-only loan is negotiated and will be repaid out of the tax-free cash from the existing self-administered pension fund.

Year 1	£
Rent receivable on £200,000 at (say) 8 per cent	16,000
Interest payable on £200,000 at (say) 12 per cent	24,000
Net deficiency to be financed out of net remuneration	(8,000)
Year 5	
Rent receivable — property value (say) £350,000 at (say) 8 per cent	28,000
Interest payable on £200,000 at (say) 12 per cent	(24,000)
Net rent received	4,000

to 30 per cent capital gains tax but at least the net cash will be received personally. The property does not have to be sold at retirement. As the property increases in value the rent is likely to exceed any interest payable and this could supplement any pension received. The property could then be used as collateral security for personal ventures. Inheritance tax business property relief may be available but if rent is received capital gains tax retirement relief at age 60 will not be given. *(See Table 3.12)*

Chapter 4
Timing Your Benefits

The age from which you can take your benefits does not necessarily coincide with the date on which you actually retire from work. You could take your benefits before you retire so that you continue to receive a salary in addition to your pension. Conversely, you could retire from work and live off your capital before taking your pension benefits. As the pension fund is a tax-free roll-up fund it may be advisable to defer taking your benefits if the scheme rules permit, as you are likely to obtain a better return this way.

It is important to consider the normal retirement age when setting up a Company scheme because the Inland Revenue's restrictions on maximum retirement benefits are all geared to the selected normal retirement age.

You will see from the example in Table 4.1 that the tax-free cash entitlement has been taken at the earliest opportunity. If under the Inland Revenue's rules you can take the maximum tax-free cash sum then as shown earlier, it will often be advisable to take it at the earliest opportunity even if the pension is not taken. However, if the maximum entitlement can only be taken if the fund continues to grow, then it may be worth delaying both the receipt of the tax-free cash sum and the pension.

Taking Benefits Early

The pension and tax-free cash can be taken as early as age 50 under Personal pension schemes and also Company

The Daily Telegraph Pensions Guide

Table 4.1

An individual aged 60 needs net income of £24,000 per annum. He has cash deposits of £200,000. His pension fund is growing at 10 per cent per annum and is now worth £500,000. His tax-free cash entitlement is £100,000.

If benefits taken at 60	Income	
	£	£
Cash deposits	200,000	
Tax-free cash	100,000	
	300,000	
Cash invested at (say) 12 per cent		36,000
Pension £400,000 at (say) 12 per cent		48,000
		84,000
Less income tax (after allowance of £3,795)		(39,781)
Net spendable income		44,219
Expenditure		(24,000)
Excess per annum		20,219
Cumulative excess for five years after return of (say) 5 per cent net		117,309

If tax-free cash taken at 60 and pension at 65	Income
	£
At 60 — income from cash deposits (as above)	36,000
Less tax (after allowances of £3,795)	(11,485)
	24,515
Expenditure	(24,000)
Excess (say) nil	515
Pension fund at 65	644,204
Pension fund at 60 (*less* tax-free cash)	(400,000)
Increase	244,204
Less cumulative investment of excess funds (as above)	117,309
Additional funds to produce income	126,895

schemes, depending on the latter's rules. Under Company schemes the accrued benefits will be reduced for early retirement. Under Personal schemes, clearly 'the more you put into the scheme the more you'll get out' so that the fund will be smaller if contributions are made to age 50 rather than if contributions and investment gains are continued beyond that age. Also subject to the movement in interest rates, annuity rates should be higher at the later date since they are based on age. However, the opportunity to take benefits at 50 will mean that for some people the benefits of the scheme will not seem so far off.

Table 4.2

A woman has been paying £2,000 per annum into a Personal pension scheme from age 30 which has been growing at 10 per cent per annum. She could take benefits at age 50 or continue funding at £2,000 per annum to 60.

	Benefits at age	
	50	60
Value of fund	£126,000	£362,000
Annuity rates applicable on retirement (say)	10 per cent	12 per cent
Pension (ignoring tax-free cash)	£12,600	£43,440

Under 'Final salary' company schemes the rules are differently applied. They can allow a member whose employment terminates before normal retirement date to take benefits from age 50 for a man or, in some cases, from age 45 for a woman. As the benefits are based upon a formula which is linked to the number of years service and final salary, the benefits will be smaller if they are taken early. An illustration of the way in which the formula could operate is shown in Table 4.3.

Table 4.3

An individual leaves his job at 50 when his final remuneration is £30,000. He had been in the Company pension scheme since the age of 30.

	Maximum pension at the age of		Tax-free cash at the age of	
	50	60	50	60
No of years service	20	30	20	30
Percentage used for each year of service	1.67	1.67	3.75	3.75
Benefits as percentage of final salary	33	50	75	112.5
Pension/tax-free cash	£10,000 per annum	£15,000 per annum	£22,500	£33,750

The above illustration is rather simplistic as since the salary is likely to increase, the final salary used in computing benefits from age 50 is likely to be smaller than at age 60. Also, there would normally be an actuarial reduction for going early, together with an increase (at 5 per cent per annum or RPI if less) in the deferred pension up to normal retirement age. These factors make it a very complicated option to evaluate and would need to be carefully considered.

Depending upon the pension scheme rules, it is possible to take the tax-free cash at normal retirement date but to delay taking the pension benefits until a later date. Taking tax-free cash earlier than the residual pension is normally advisable. However, you could be giving up good pension increases by doing so and should take advice. The decision may also be influenced by your state of health and the commutation factor used by the scheme.

Special cases

Under Personal or Company pension schemes, the pension may be paid earlier than age 50 if the individual is incapacitated. The pension payable will be based upon the amount in the fund in the case of a Money purchase or PPS arrangement and the member's age. This may be increased above the normal rate if the life expectancy is shorter than normal. Under Company schemes, if the retirement is caused by incapacity the pension and lump sum is usually a fraction the member could have received had he remained in service until normal retirement date. The definitions of incapacity for Personal pension and Company schemes are similar and are set out in Appendix 5.

Under a Final salary scheme, if an employee is in 'exceptional circumstances of ill health', then the entire pension can be commuted for a cash sum but the excess over the normal lump sum would be subject to tax at 10 per cent.

There are several occupations in which it is normal to retire from Personal schemes before 50 and which have been approved by the Inland Revenue; the benefits can be taken at an earlier date even though under certain arrangements the benefits may be reduced. A summary of these occupations is set out in Appendix 6.

Taking Benefits Late

If you are in the fortunate position of not having to rely upon your pension when you reach normal retirement age, it may be worthwhile 'rolling up' the scheme and deferring the benefits. As mentioned earlier, it will normally be advisable to take the tax-free cash at an early date if this is within your control; however, the pension could be deferred so as to produce a greater fund and a larger pension when it is needed as explained earlier in this chapter. The decision will depend upon your final salary, tax situation, other income and financial requirements. The pension benefits can only be deferred until you are 75 at which time they must be taken. Unfortunately it is not possible to defer part of your pension — it is an 'all or nothing situation'. You either take your pension or defer it completely. Another advantage of deferring benefits is to save inheritance tax as explained in the section dealing with Death-in-service benefits.

For those in a Money purchase arrangement, the timing of benefits is important. It may be advisable to wait, if interest and annuity rates are likely to increase. For example, those retiring in April 1987 will have been up to 15 per cent worse off than those retiring three months earlier due to falling annuity rates.

Chapter 5
State Pensions

National Insurance Contributions

If you are a director or employee then national insurance contributions (NICs) will be deducted from your salary, and your employer is also required to make NICs to provide for your State pension. The level of contributions which will be

---

Table 5.1

A woman earns a salary of £10,000 per annum and is a member of a contracted-in Company pension scheme.

	£	£
Class I NIC payable by employee at 9 per cent	–	900
Class I NIC payable by employer at 10.45 per cent		1,045
NIC payable if she had been self-employed		1,945
Class 2 £3.85 × 52	–	200
Class 4 £5,410 (£10,000 − 4,590) × 6.3 per cent	341	
Tax relief £341 × 27 per cent × 1/2	(46)	295
		495

59

payable depends upon whether or not the employer has contracted out of the State scheme. This is considered in more detail later in the book, and the contributions are set out in Appendix 7. The Appendix also includes the rates applicable to the self-employed and the voluntary contribution which may be payable to ensure that maximum State benefits are received. You will see from Table 5.1 that the contributions are more expensive for employed people.

The employee's contribution will not attract tax relief but the employer's contribution will be tax allowable. The earnings upon which NIC is charged has a maximum ceiling of £15,340 per annum for employees and directors. However, this ceiling was removed for employers. This action was really another way of imposing a tax charge as the contributions payable by employers on earnings of over £15,340 were not originally required to produce State pensions. The charge can be substantial especially if directors are receiving a high level of remuneration.

The employee trust has been used as a means of paying remuneration to directors without an employers' NIC

Table 5.2

A director receives remuneration of £200,000 per annum and is a member of a Contracted-out pension scheme.

	£
NIC payable by director	
£39 × 9 per cent × 52	183
£256 × 6.85 per cent × 52	912
£295	1,095
NIC payable by company	
£256 × 52 = £13,312 × 6.35 per cent	845
£186,688 × 10.45 per cent	19,509
£200,000	20,354

charge. However, this route will no longer be available from October 1987. Directors may want to receive their remuneration by way of a dividend in future, although the company's corporation tax position will need to be considered as well as the other share valuation and apportionment ramifications. Also the payment of a dividend rather than a salary could reduce pension benefits and this will need to be carefully borne in mind.

The NIC contributions are used to finance the State pension scheme. The scheme is in two tiers; the basic retirement pension and the State Earnings Related Pension Scheme (SERPS).

The Basic Retirement Pension

Provided a man pays full NICs for 44 years and a woman pays full rate contributions for 39 years, the State will provide a retirement pension of currently £2,054 per annum (£39.50 per week) at age 65 for men and 60 for women. A husband and wife will each receive this pension if they have both made full NICs as described above. If the husband only has made contributions then the pension for a married couple will be £3,289 (£63.25 per week). The above State pensions may be reduced if a man under 70 or a woman under 65 continues to work after normal retirement age and earns more than £3,900 per annum (£75 per week). The State also provides a widow's pension, and this and certain other State benefits are set out in Appendix 8.

The State Earnings Related Pension Scheme (SERPS)

For the majority of taxpayers, the basic retirement pension will be totally inadequate to cover their annual expenditure.

In 1978 SERPS was introduced as a means of 'topping-up' the basic pension and is funded by the additional NICs which contracted-in employees pay on earnings between the lower and upper limits, which are currently £2,028 to £15,340 per annum. Under the existing scheme, the pension accrues at a rate of 1.25 per cent per annum up to a maximum level of 25 per cent, although the proportion accumulated is dependent upon your working life (ie best 20 years for maximum benefit) with each accrual being index-linked.

Table 5.3

An individual receives a fixed salary of £11,000 per annum for the 20 years up to retirement age. Assuming the lower NIC threshold was £2,028 per annum throughout, the SERPS pension would be as follows (ignoring the index-linked increment).

	£ per annum
Salary	11,000
Less lower NIC limit	(2,028)
	8,972
Annual pension accrual at 1.25 per cent	112.15
SERPS pension £112.15 × 20	2,243
Basic pension (say) married couple rate	3,289
Total pension	5,532

The SERPS pension will be index-linked and the widow will continue to receive the pension from her husband's death. The SERPS will normally depend upon the way in which the employee's earnings have increased over the 20 years before retirement and the level of inflation over that period. If the employee retired on a salary of £11,000 per annum and his salary increased in line with inflation over that period, then the SERPS Pension of £2,243 as shown in Table 5.3 would not require any adjustment. However, as

State Pensions

the SERPS scheme was not introduced until 1978, any employee retiring in the next decade will not get the full benefit as the SERPS benefit will only have accrued since 1978 and the greatly reduced graduated pension will be received in respect of the earnings period before 1975. Also, SERPS is modified by the following changes:

1. People retiring from 2009 will receive a SERPS pension based on 20 per cent of lifetime earnings ('the new basis') rather than 25 per cent of the best 20 of these years ('the old basis'). The pay definition will be based on lifetime earnings and not the best 20 years.

2. For people retiring before 2009, the pension will be based upon a combination of the old basis up to 6 April 1988 and the new basis thereafter.

3. Provision will be made to protect the SERPS pension of people unable to work because they are looking after a child or a disabled person or are themselves disabled.

4. Widows and widowers over 65 will inherit half their spouses' SERPS pension rather than all of it. However, this change will not affect people widowed before year 2000.

The change in percentage terms of a person's SERPS pension for somebody aged 40 will now be to reduce the SERPS pension from 25 per cent of the relevant earnings to approximately 21 per cent. The long-term effect will be a 50 per cent cut-back for the State in providing the SERPS pension.

Chapter 6
Guidelines for Employers

The previous chapters have concentrated on areas which are mainly of concern to the individual. The remainder of the book covers matters which will be of particular interest to the employer. It is important that employers review their pension arrangements (if any) for directors and staff, appreciate which changes affect them and consider the available options because of the changes which are now taking place. If they do not, then they could be missing financial opportunities and may be unprepared for action which their employees may take.

The following chapters will outline the changes in more detail but the rest of this chapter is devoted to the points which employers should be addressing. It is by no means an exhaustive list.

Contracting-out

All employers will be able to contract out of SERPS, the State scheme, from April 1988. Previously, only employers with a Final salary scheme could contract-out but from April 1988 Money purchase arrangements can be used for this purpose. By contracting-out the employer will not only take on the liability of the SERPS pension but will also benefit from reduced national insurance charges. The decision as to whether the employer should contract-out will require careful consideration. Employers must be confident that the benefits will outweigh the liabilities. Urgent advice on this matter will be required because if action is delayed certain benefits may be lost.

The Choice of Schemes

Only half the UK's workforce are in a pension scheme which goes with their job. Approximately 10 million employees are currently relying upon the State to provide their pension. As the State pension was not designed to replace earnings but merely supplement the lost income, many of those employees are likely to be in financial difficulty in retirement.

Employers tend to fall into various categories. There are those who will never set up a pension scheme for their staff and tend to begrudge the salary they have to pay. There are those who would like to set up a scheme but are concerned at the additional administration involved (a simplified Money purchase or Group personal pension scheme could be appropriate in their case). Others would like to set up a scheme and are not unduly concerned at the administration involved. Some are constantly looking for ways to improve their scheme while others have improved the benefits and are happy that no further action is required.

Those employers who are seeking methods of retaining good staff recognise that a good pension scheme is one of the most popular and tax-efficient perks for directors and staff alike. The workforce of certain industries are more stable than other sectors which suffer from a higher staff turnover. In the latter case, employees may prefer cash bonuses to a good pension scheme, but if the pension problems which are associated with job mobility are overcome then a Company pension scheme may be more attractive and become more commonplace.

Guidelines for Employers

The interest in pensions is increasing. Employers without a pension scheme should consider the benefits to be gained from introducing one and, of course, the costs involved. Those who already have a scheme should consider whether they wish to improve the existing benefits.

The employer who wishes to introduce a pension scheme is faced with a number of bewildering choices as to which of the following would be the most appropriate:

(a) Money purchase scheme; or
(b) Final salary scheme; or
(c) New simplified arrangements; or
(d) Executive 'top hat' scheme; or
(e) Self-administered scheme; or
(f) Hybrid scheme; or
(g) contributions to an employee's own Personal pension scheme.

These different arrangements are described in more detail later in the book. If an employer decides to introduce or improve a scheme then the benefits should be explained to the staff. Pensions are a complicated subject so do not assume that employees will immediately appreciate the advantages of the new system. Ironically, you could find them wholly unappreciative in spite of all the trouble to which you have been.

There are a range of benefits which can be provided by the employer and employee. Normally the overriding factor will be the cost of these benefits. The employer will need to choose which benefits are to be provided in order of priority and keep within his budget. These can include an escalating pension at retirement, a widow's pension, life assurance protection etc. Employers will also need to consider how the changing rules relating to the definition of 'final remuneration' would affect key executives in the future.

Additional Voluntary Contributions

In the past employees often did not make use of the Additional Voluntary Contributions (AVC) facility. This may have been because the scheme rules did not cater for such payments or the employee did not want to be committed to future contributions at the same rate. Although new AVC arrangements will not produce tax-free cash, the changes should make AVCs more attractive, especially as they can be 'free standing'. Employers will need to consider carefully the action which they need to take in relation to their own AVC scheme in view of the introduction of the new free-standing AVC arrangements in October 1987.

Employers may wish to make their staff aware of the new AVC arrangements as many can now improve their pension benefits by personal contributions at no cost to the employer. This could make the employee more aware of the existing benefits of the employer's scheme and could shift part of the burden of improving the benefits on to the employee. However, the employee may wish to write his 'free-standing' contract with another investment house. This could be against the paternalistic wishes of the employer who may prefer to see his employees' pension arrangements staying within the Company's scheme and the existing finance house.

Job Mobility

One of the main aims of the Government is to make it easier for employees to change jobs. This can be a double-edged sword for employers. Those wishing to attract new staff should welcome any such changes, while those who have problems in retaining staff may be worried by the changes.

Employers have been more concerned at preserving

benefits for those employees who remain within schemes rather than helping those who leave. Employers can still make it more difficult for leavers by the way in which the leaving benefits are computed according to the scheme rules. In the current climate of improved job mobility and increasing awareness of pensions, employers will need to consider carefully how they structure leavers' benefits.

The New Personal Pension Scheme

The new Personal Pension Scheme (PPS) era is likely to bring with it a number of problems for employers. The general awareness of the benefits which may be derived from schemes has been relatively poor due mainly to the complexity of scheme rules. A number of different parties will now be promoting pensions in general and the new PPS in particular, so the general awareness of pension arrangements should improve. It is often said that a little knowledge can be dangerous and those involved with the PPS will be promoting it for different reasons.

The Government will promote it as part of the overall plan for reducing the State's burden to provide for pensions, while the direct sales forces of life companies and other financial institutions see it as a great market for business. But will it be a good thing for the employer?

If an employer has no pension scheme, the employees may now be willing to set up their own plan. This, in principle, is not a bad idea but there is likely to be more pressure from the employees for their employers to help provide for their retirement. It may be better for the employer to take the initiative and set up an Occupational scheme on the employer's (and not the employee's) terms.

If an employer does have an existing scheme, the employees may wish to opt out of it and set up their own

PPS. This may be detrimental to them but if they are not separately advised, they may be guided by the publicity and advertising relating to the new PPS and not fully understand the implications of such action. Clearly, if there is mass migration from a scheme by the younger members, the structure of the fund will be significantly affected.

The employer may need to get his message across to the employees and illustrate the benefits of the existing scheme and the dangers of leaving it. The most powerful weapon for employers is to refuse to contribute to a PPS which will benefit those employees who remain in the Occupational scheme. Therefore, the employer's stance could be to continue to fund for benefits for those who remain within the existing scheme but not contribute (or do so at a reduced rate) to the PPS of those who opt out. Clearly, preventative action to avoid these problems is preferable. If an employee does contract out of the Occupational scheme then the employer should consider whether that employee will have sufficient life cover, and may consider insuring the employee's life to cover any moral obligation to protect his family on his premature death.

Management of the Funds

Another important choice the employer faces is in selecting the finance house which will manage the funds. As will be seen later in this book, the difference in investment performance between different fund managers is extremely varied. The effect on the funding levels can be very dramatic. For example, many schemes have become over-funded because of the bull markets in the 1980s. Good fund management also contributed to many Final salary pension schemes becoming over-funded. This can relieve the employer of the burden of making pension contributions for several years. On the other hand, a badly managed fund can put a severe financial strain on the employer. This is why good impartial advice on the selection of the fund and fund managers is essential.

Chapter 7
Contracting-out

The problem faced by this country is outlined in the leaflet 'Saving for Retirement — Pension' which was published by the DHSS in September 1986. It stated that only half the workforce is now in job-related pension schemes. The rest must be in SERPS to 'top-up' their State pension which will be paid from the NIC of those who are in work.

The Government believes that SERPS is making generous promises which contributors of the next century may not in practice be able to meet as no fund is building up to meet those pledges. It is estimated that by the year 2033 there will be about *four million more pensioners than there are today* while the workforce (who will have to ensure that the pensions are paid) is likely to fall in number. Without a radical restructuring of the system it is estimated that the workforce would face a bill of over £25,000 million on top of the cost of the basic State pension — far more than the entire cost of paying pensions today. The proposed changes to SERPS will reduce this cost to about £13,000 million.

It is against this background that the changes to SERPS are to be made. While a pension scheme is contracted in to the State scheme, NICs for employees who are not contracted out of SERPS will continue to fund for the SERPS pension. However, if an employer contracts out of the State scheme then the burden of paying the SERPS pension *moves from the State to the employer*. It is for this reason that a number of incentives are now being made to entice employers and employees to 'contract-out' of the State scheme. If a scheme is to be 'contracted-out' it must pay at least the Guaranteed Minimum Pension (GMP), which is an amount approximately equal to the 'earnings related' element of the State pension scheme. The GMP includes the entitlement to a widow's pension and an element of index-linking, which would have been the case under SERPS so that the employee's position does not suffer. There is to be a new basis for contracting out from April 1988, which does not involve GMPs.

State Benefits

As we have seen earlier, for most people the State pension (including SERPS) is unlikely to be sufficient to maintain an adequate standard of living in retirement. This is particularly the case for those whose earnings are above the top NIC threshold of £15,340 per annum, as SERPS only provides a pension on earnings up to that threshold. The SERPS pension is based on 20 to 25 per cent of those earnings and, the 'rule of thumb' calculation is that two-thirds of your salary will be required in retirement to avoid a drop in living standards. Table 7.1 can be used as a simple guide to the

---

Table 7.1

A married man earning £20,000 per annum retires at 65. He has paid the maximum NIC contributions under SERPS and it is assumed that his salary increased in line with inflation and that the NIC thresholds have remained constant throughout.

	£
State pension — basic	3,289
— SERPS at current maximum rate £13,312 (£15,340-2,028) at 25 per cent	3,328
Total State pension (33 per cent of final salary)	6,617
Required pension £20,000 at 67 per cent	13,400

maximum benefits which an employee could receive from the State pension. It assumes that earnings, inflation and investment returns have been constant (an unlikely scenario).

NIC Benefits

One of the incentives of contracting out of the State scheme is that the NICs which are paid by the employer and employee are reduced. This is because part of the NICs are no longer required as the employer rather than the State will now pay SERPS pension. The rates are set out in Appendix 7 and an illustration of the savings are set out in the following table.

Table 7.2

NI contributions		Earnings of employee			
		£5,000	£10,000	£15,000	£20,000
		£	£	£	£
Employer	— contracted in	350	1,045	1,567	2,090
	— contracted out	(228)	(718)	(1,036)	(1,544)
	— saving	122	327	531	546
Employee	— contracted in	350	900	1,350	1,381
	— contracted out	(286)	(729)	(1,071)	(1,094)
	— saving	64	171	279	287
Total	— contracted in	700	1,945	2,917	3,471
	— contracted out	(514)	(1,447)	(2,107)	(2,638)
	— saving	186	498	810	833

The NIC benefits to an employer will depend upon the size of the workforce and the size of salaries.

Table 7.3

A company employs 1,000 people whose average earnings are £15,000 per annum.

	NIC payable by company £
Under contracted-in scheme approx.	1,567,000
Under contracted-out scheme approx.	(1,036,000)
NIC saving	531,000
Less corporation tax relief at (say) 35 per cent approx.	(186,000)
Net saving of NICs on contracting out	345,000

If the employer arranges for his Money purchase scheme to be contracted out of SERPS from April 1988 then he will be required to pay the total rebate in NICs into the pension scheme. The minimum payments required will be equivalent to the difference between the standard rate and contracted-out rate NICs on those earnings. He will be entitled to recoup the employee's share of this from his earnings. As a consequence, it will be possible for an employer to set up a Money purchase contracted-out pension scheme at no cost whatsoever to the employer, although such a scheme will only provide a low level of benefits.

The '2 per cent' Incentive Payment

As an additional incentive to relieve the State of providing for SERPS, the DHSS will make an additional contribution into certain contracted-out pension schemes. As it relates to the SERPS pension, which is funded from NICs on remuneration between the lower and upper earnings limits (currently £2,028 to £15,340), the annual 2 per cent incentive payment (minimum £1 per week) will also be based on these earnings. The incentive payment will normally be payable over a five-year period from 6 April 1988 to 5 April 1993, but for employees taking out a PPS on or after 1 July 1988 it could be back-dated to 6 April 1987. It will produce additional benefits in a Money purchase scheme, while in the case of a Final salary scheme it will effectively reduce the employer's costs as the benefit rates are pre-determined. The payment is made by the DHSS directly into the employee's pension fund; it will not be received directly by the employee or employer. The incentive payment could be substantial in respect of large pension schemes.

Table 7.4

Facts as per the previous example.

	Benefit per annum £	Benefits over the five-year period £
Net annual NIC benefit from contracting out	345,000	1,725,000
2 per cent incentive payment to pension fund of employees £12,972 (£15,000 −2,028) × 2 per cent = £259.44 × 1,000 approx.	259,440	1,297,200
Total benefits	604,440	3,022,200

The incentive payment will be appropriate in the following cases.

1. *Schemes for employees*
Schemes which have contracted-out of SERPS since 1 January 1986 will be able to qualify for the incentive payment. It will not be paid if the scheme was already contracted-out of SERPS before 1 January 1986.

2. *Personal pension schemes (PPS)*
Employees or directors who take out a Personal pension plan and use this to contract-out of SERPS can also qualify for the incentive payment. The incentive payment will not be made, however, if the employee's job had been contracted-out of SERPS for at least two years from the notification date. The employer's permission may be required if the employee wishes to contract out before 5 April 1988.

If notification of contracting-out is made before the end of a tax year, the entitlement to the incentive payment will be back-dated to the previous 5 April (but not normally paid until the following October). Although the starting date for Personal pension scheme arrangements has been delayed from 4 January to 1 July 1988, the employee can take out a contracted-out Personal pension scheme from 1 July 1988 and this would entitle the employee to the incentive payment for the period of six years from 1987/88, not the five years originally announced by the Government.

The incentive payment will not be applicable to the self-employed who pay a different range of NIC rates. If an individual contracts out of the State scheme and sets up his own PPS, the following contributions will be made by the DHSS if an appropriate scheme certificate has been obtained from the Occupational Pensions Board.

1. The contracting-out rebate in respect of the employer's and employee's NIC.
2. Basic-rate income tax relief in respect of the employee's contracting-out rebate.

3. The special incentive payment of 2 per cent if appropriate.

The payments will be made directly by the DHSS and will automatically allow for basic-rate income tax relief on the employee's share of the contracting-out rebate. The grossed-up equivalent of the employer's rebate will be treated as income of and contributions paid by the individual so that the tax effect should be neutral to a basic-rate taxpayer. It is currently understood that the employee will need to claim any higher-rate tax relief when his tax return is submitted. This relief may be overlooked unless the employee is aware of the procedure. However, this procedure has yet to be clarified.

Table 7.5

An employee earning £40,000 per annum and whose marginal rate of income tax is 60 per cent contracts out of the State scheme and sets up his own PPS. Ignoring any other pension contribution the position using 1987/88 rates would be as follows.

Payments by DHSS

	£	£
Employer's rebate £13,312 × 4.10 per cent	–	546
Employee's rebate £13,312 × 2.15 per cent	286	–
Basic-rate tax credit £286 × 27/73	106	–
		392
Incentive payment £13,312 × 2 per cent	–	266
Total payments by DHSS		1,204

The accumulated fund from these payments must be used to buy a pension for the member at age 65 for men and 60 for women. No tax-free cash may be taken from these contributions. However, the following provisions must also be made from the fund to produce 'protected rights':

1. A spouse's pension on death before retirement in certain circumstances, if the widow or widower has dependent children or is aged over 44 or under other special circumstances.
2. A spouse's pension of 50 per cent of the member's rate on death after retirement.
3. Pension increases at 3 per cent per annum (or the increase in the RPI if less).

The Employer's Decision

There are two main types of pension scheme: the Final salary scheme and the Money purchase arrangement. Both of these are explained later in the book. In the past it was only possible for a Final salary scheme to contract-out of SERPS so that, until now, Money purchase arrangements have not been able to contract-out.

Many small employers have not been able to contract-out in the past as they fought shy of taking on the open-ended commitment of a Final salary scheme and may have set up a Money purchase arrangement. Final salary schemes which have not previously contracted-out will now be able to do so and the Money purchase schemes will be able to do so from 6 April 1988.

By contracting-out, the employer will be taking on the State's liability to pay the SERPS pension. As most Final salary schemes will already be providing a pension of this level, they are normally contracted-out. However, those Final salary schemes which are still contracted-in and all Money purchase schemes will probably need to take action to contract-out under the simplified rules from April 1988.

Contracting-out

However, care will be required to ensure that the employer is not taking on a net liability by contracting-out. The following table illustrates the position from the perspective of an individual who has a choice of remaining in a Final salary scheme or contracting-out through a Personal pension.

Table 7.6

Pension — as a percentage of final pay

Age in April 1988	SERPS pension	Personal pension (a)	Personal pension (b)	Final salary scheme
	%	%	%	%
25	13	14	22	67
30	12	13	18	58
35	12	11	15	50
40	11	10	13	42
45	11	8	10	33
50	10	7	8	25
55	8	5	6	17
60	4	3	3	8

Notes:
1. All the above figures relate to a man earning £10,000 per annum in April 1988 and are expressed as a percentage of the man's projected earnings at retirement.
2. The figures under 'SERPS pension' show the amount by which the individual's SERPS would be reduced if he were to take out a contracted-out Personal pension scheme on 1 July 1988.
3. The figures under the 'Personal pension' columns relate to the pension which can be purchased by the minimum contributions to a contracted-out Personal pension scheme from 1 July 1988.

The contributions to the Personal pension scheme are as follows:
(a) the rebate in the contracted-out NICs (5.8 per cent of earnings between the lower and upper earnings limits), including an allowance for the rebate to reduce (to an assumed rate of 3.8 per cent of earnings from 2028 onwards);

(b) a tax credit in respect of the employee's share of the rebate in NICs;
(c) an incentive payment of 2 per cent of earnings between the lower and upper earnings limits for the period from April 1988 to March 1993.

The calculations have been carried out using the following assumptions:
— an investment return of (a) 8 per cent per annum and (b) 10 per cent per annum;
— increases in earnings and the lower and upper earnings limits of 8 per cent per annum;
— expenses of 10 per cent of the contributions.

4. The figures under 'Final salary scheme' relate to the expected pension in respect of membership of a scheme from 1 July 1988 which provides a retirement pension of 1/60 of final salary for each year of membership.

You will see that for a male, contracting out of the State scheme will generally be advantageous if he is young, but may not be wise if he is nearing retirement; therefore, the average age of the Group scheme is important. The pension which will be produced by a contracted-out Money purchase scheme is dependent upon the investment returns. In recent years these have exceeded the rate of inflation but in the 1970s the trend was reversed. The Final salary scheme will normally provide for benefits in excess of SERPS so that, as mentioned above, most Final salary schemes will be contracted out.

The Employee's Decision

If you are an employee you would generally have no control over whether your employer contracts out the Group scheme but you could leave the scheme and set up your own Personal pension arrangement. However, as demonstrated in the previous example, this could be an unwise move unless your employer contributes to the new scheme at a reasonable level. Also, a Final salary scheme may provide you with better benefits so that you could be jeopardising your position by taking this action. Professional advice should be taken before proceeding any further.

Chapter 8
Occupational Pension Schemes

Occupational pension schemes are those set up by an employer for its directors and/or employees. The new Personal pension schemes can only be set up by employees even though employers can contribute to them and are dealt with separately in this book.

In the second half of this century, Occupational pension schemes have become more commonplace, complicated and sophisticated. A man who has worked for a company all his life can expect to receive a payment upon retirement and the employer will often feel obliged to make the payment which can encourage the employee to take life easier and make way for a younger man. If the company has not made provision for this event, then it can suffer financially in a year in which many of the staff retire. The provision of a pension scheme recognises the moral obligation of ensuring that staff have more than the State pension in retirement. And the establishment of a pension fund recognises the financial obligation of paying for the supplementary pension in advance.

The Company pension scheme is now a normal part of the salary package. However, some companies will have started in a small way and in the early years, when they were struggling to establish themselves, the directors may not have felt the need to set up a scheme for their staff, especially if they were well-remunerated. After this start-up period, the directors may accept the need for a scheme and will then require advice on how to fund the scheme as there are various alternatives, which are outlined in this book.

Special restrictions apply to 20 per cent owners and controlling directors as far as Inland Revenue limits are concerned and these are set out in Appendix 9.

Money Purchase Schemes

A Money purchase scheme is relatively simple for the employer and employee to understand. The principle involved is 'the more you put in, the more you get out'. Careful thought is required from the outset to determine the contribution levels of the scheme. For example, the directors may agree to set up a scheme and contribute, say, 8 per cent of the employee's salary only if that employee pays, say, 4 per cent into the scheme. Each year the directors will be able to compute the pension cost as the amount payable is pre-determined. If the salary payroll is £100,000 then the company will pay £8,000 based on an 8 per cent contribution level. Each member's benefits are those which are acquired by the contributions which are made for and by him so that he is unaffected by the other members of the scheme. As each member can have his own 'account' under this arrangement, less input is needed from the actuary and the

---

Table 8.1

A man retires at 65 on a salary of £30,000. He joined the Company scheme at 45 and has received salary increases at an average rate of 5 per cent per annum. Contributions have been made at 14 per cent of salary and the fund has grown at an average rate of 10 per cent per annum.

	£
Final salary	30,000
Value of fund at 65	141,883
Pension for life assuming 12 per cent annuity rate	17,026

scheme is easier to administer. The pension receivable by the member will depend upon the amount paid into the scheme and the returns (after expenses) which have been achieved from investing the money.

While the Money purchase scheme is easy for the employer to understand, it suffers from a lack of guarantee as the benefits will be reduced if the investment performance of the fund is poor. Also the benefit is very dependent upon the annuity rates on retirement. The company is not liable to supplement the pension if it is less than was originally projected. Money purchase schemes, however, tend to benefit staff who join a scheme at a young age and those who change jobs regularly.

Final Salary Schemes

This type of scheme recognises that the highest salary is normally earned in the period immediately before retirement. Apart from controlling directors of companies, most employees cannot regulate their salary to suit their pension requirements and are unlikely to have falling remuneration upon retirement if they have remained in full-time employment. The 'rule of thumb' requirement for a

---

Table 8.2

Three individuals retire at age 60 on a final salary of £30,000. Their pensions will vary according to their length of service.

Final salary of £30,000	*Length of service before retirement*		
	20 years	*30 years*	*40 years*
	£ per annum	£ per annum	£ per annum
Pensions payable	10,000	15,000	20,000

retirement income of two-thirds of final salary reflects the need to base your pension on your pre-retirement salary. Unlike the Money purchase arrangement, this form of scheme recognises this and promises that the pension will be a percentage of your final salary. The relevant percentage of final salary is normally related to the time spent in the company's employment. Each pension scheme will be different, but many schemes use a multiple of 1/60 so that if you work for a company for 40 years up to retirement age your pension will be two-thirds (ie 40/60) of final salary. Also there are many different definitions of 'final salary' for this purpose — often the salary is averaged over the last year, or three years, before retirement.

By setting up a Final salary scheme, the employer is committed to a contribution level which will produce a fund to meet the promises which have been made. This complex funding arrangement will require a guiding hand from an actuary. (Most independent intermediaries will be able to put you in touch with one.) Before setting up such a scheme and setting the level of pension benefits from the scheme, an employer needs an estimate of how much it will cost to provide the promised benefits. Unlike the Money purchase scheme, the employee does not usually have a readily identifiable 'account' but is part of a group arrangement. The employer's contribution rate will be an average to cover the total liabilities of the scheme, so that the pension contributions in respect of the younger members could be subsidising the benefits paid to the older members.

The factors which would influence the funding arrangements include the following:

(a) the company's payroll;
(b) the ages and sex of the members;
(c) the increase in salaries in future years;
(d) the level of growth and inflation in future years;
(e) the level of benefits under the scheme;

Occupational Pension Schemes

(f) the number of employees leaving the scheme before retirement;
(g) the eligibility conditions for the scheme;
(h) the expenses of the scheme.

As mentioned above, the Final salary scheme may produce a higher pension than the Money purchase scheme as illustrated by the following example.

Table 8.3

Salary on entrance into pension scheme £10,000. Average salary increase of 10 per cent for 20 years to retirement and an average growth rate of 12 per cent. A man retires on £67,275 at 65. His wife is younger. The pension escalates at 5 per cent per annum (annuity rate in this case is 9 per cent).

Money purchase scheme

Funding rate (employer 8 per cent/employee 4 per cent)	12%
Value of fund at retirement	£196,143
Pension for life	£17,653

Final salary scheme

Pension benefits 20/60 of final salary	£22,425
Value of fund required	£249,167
Average funding rate	15.2%

You will see that the two schemes use a different funding approach. The Money purchase scheme has a predetermined funding level of 12 per cent of the salary cost. Therefore the fund value will depend upon the investment gains which, in this case, have produced a fund of £196,143. The Final salary scheme has promised a pension of £22,425 per annum based on the final salary and a fund of £249,167 must be built up to pay for it. The actuary is needed every three years (sometimes more frequently) to check that the scheme can meet its ongoing liabilities. It has had to fund at a higher rate than the Money purchase scheme to make up the balance of £53,024 (£249,167 − 196,143) representing the additional fund required to meet the cost of the benefits which it has promised its member.

In recent years, the bull market has resulted in a number of Final salary schemes being over-funded, and the fund producing more money than that needed to meet its liabilities. The effect on Money purchase schemes has been simply to improve benefits.

One of the main problems with the Final salary scheme occurs when a member changes job and leaves the scheme as shown by the following example.

Table 8.4

Facts as per the previous example, but the employee changes job and leaves the scheme after five years.

	£
Money purchase scheme	
Value of fund at leaving	10,203
Projected fund at age 65	55,847
Pension for life	6,702
Final salary scheme	
Leaving salary after five years	16,105
Deferred pension benefits £16,105 × 5/60	1,342
Assuming an escalation factor of 5 per cent per annum until retirement — final pension	2,790

From the previous two examples you will see that although the Final pay scheme is better than the Money purchase scheme should the member stay to retirement, the opposite applies if the member leaves after, say, five years.

Occupational Pension Schemes

A summary of the main differences of a Final salary scheme as compared with a Money purchase scheme is set out below:

(a) it is more difficult to understand;
(b) it is normally more expensive to run and requires more input from an actuary;
(c) the liability of the employer is unlimited and not governed by a fixed rate;
(d) the scheme normally produces a better pension for the employee who does not change job.

In addition, Hybrid schemes exist which are a combination of Final salary and Money purchase arrangements.

The New Simplified Arrangements

The Government recognises that the setting up of a pension scheme can be a formidable and costly undertaking. Its current intention, however, is to encourage the privatisation of pensions and so new simplified schemes are to be available from April 1988.

A new simplified Money purchase arrangement will be introduced, the main features of which will be:

(a) an overall limit on contributions of up to 17.5 per cent of earnings, with the same percentage applying to all members; and
(b) no limit on total retirement benefits; and
(c) the tax-free lump sum should not exceed 25 per cent of the fund subject to an overall limit of £150,000.

Standard scheme documentation will be available to speed up Inland Revenue approval. In order to achieve these simplifications the following restrictions will be imposed:

(a) members cannot also participate in other Occupational schemes (except those only offering Death-in-service or widow's benefits); and
(b) controlling directors (owning over 20 per cent of the company's shares) will be excluded from membership; and
(c) only contracted-out Money purchase schemes can be self-administered.

Simplified Final salary schemes will also be available, the main features of which will be as follows:

(a) basic pension benefits will accrue at a maximum of 1/80 final salary for each year of service, up to 40 (ie maximum 50 per cent final salary);
(b) the basic tax-free lump sum will be 3/120 final salary for each year of service, up to 40 (ie 100 per cent final salary); and
(c) AVCs may be paid (by employer or employee) to bring the pension benefit up to 1/60 final salary (maximum 2/3), and the tax-free lump sum up to 3/80 final salary (maximum 150 per cent).

These benefits may be less attractive to employees (but possibly more attractive to employers!) than under other Final salary schemes which provide for maximum benefits without the need for the AVC. Again, standard documentation should be available and the complicated rules relating to accelerated accrual will not be needed. Also, scheme administrators will not have to take 'retained benefits' from earlier employments into account when calculating benefits.

As you will see, the benefits are very basic. In practice, the main benefit from the simplified Money purchase arrangement is that it will not be necessary to employ an actuary to review the funding levels as there will be no limit on benefits. Although the documentation should be simplified, most life offices and pensions brokers already use standard documentation which covers the various pension scheme arrangements and which has been approved by the Inland Revenue so that the simplified documentation should not be regarded as a major benefit. It is difficult to see the role for simplified Final salary schemes except, possibly, for Industry-wide pensions schemes.

If the contribution levels will never exceed 17.5 per cent of earnings, then the simplified Money purchase arrangements could be used. However, you would not be able to 'top-up' benefits above these levels and this could be extremely restrictive in the future. You should take care before proceeding under the new simplified arrangements.

Industry-Wide Schemes

As most job changes are likely to take place within an industry with, for example, a chemical engineer transferring from one job in that sector to another, it is proposed by the Government that Industry-wide schemes should be introduced. A scheme can therefore be designed for several employers so that a job move will not interrupt scheme membership and should ease administration for employers. Moreover, the present requirement that for tax-free lump sum purposes the calculation has to take account of each 'slice' of service with individual employers will not apply to simplified schemes. Further details of these arrangements should be available in due course.

The Government has stated that it remains committed to encouraging groups of employers to pool arrangements for providing pensions. This should reduce their administrative costs and help job mobility between employers in the group. Examples of Industry-wide schemes are schemes for the motor agents' association and solicitors' staff.

Small Self-Administered Schemes

You may have heard of the term 'Small self-administered pension scheme'. This term normally refers to schemes consisting of less than 12 members. These could more aptly be called self-managed schemes as the investment of the funds may be managed by the members. A Company scheme with a large number of members will, as you would expect, normally be managed by an investment house. It would not be prudent for the funds to be invested by the company directors as the scheme may require daily management by those who have both the experience and expertise of fund management. However, there are advantages in schemes for directors of private companies to be effectively managed by the members themselves. Also, although much more restricted, there are some Personal pension schemes operated by insurance companies which will allow the member self-management. This is the only Self-management option available to partners or sole traders.

Self-administered schemes are often attractive to directors who have more confidence in their own entrepreneurial investment flair than that of an institution and for people who have specific investment plans. The fund can be used to assist the company by, for example, acquiring new business premises or loaning up to 50 per cent of the fund back to the company, but this will need to be for a specific commercial purpose and a commercial return will need to be received. When the fund is large, the costs may be cheaper than under insured arrangements. However, the cost of appointing specialists to provide actuarial reports and the services of pensioneer trustees etc will need to be taken into account. The cost of setting up and operating a self-administered scheme could be relatively high until the contribution levels reach approximately £20,000 per annum.

While it may seem attractive for directors to be able to control the destiny of their own fund, many do not have the time or expertise to worry about the investment strategy which may need to be delegated to specialists. However, certain directors like the flexibility of being able to take back control of the investment of the funds at some time in the future. This is why even if the funds are to be managed from the outset, it may be advisable to set up the scheme under a self-administered umbrella so that investment control may be acquired by the members in the future.

The Superannuation Funds Office of the Inland Revenue (SFO) explained their approach to Small self-administered pension schemes in memorandum No 58 which was issued in February 1979. It stated that the:

> . . . more critical approach adopted by the SFO in individual cases has followed inevitably from proposals which seem designed either for tax avoidance or to benefit the employer's business financially, rather than as straightforward arrangements for providing financial support for the members in old age . . . Obviously it is not for the Inland Revenue to interfere in the way the trustees invest trust monies, except where tax avoidance is in point or where investment appears to be irreconcilable with the bona fides of the scheme having regard to its cash needs for purchasing annuities. Investment in land or buildings may be a good long-term investment for a scheme where the members are many years from retirement, but even so, questions would need to be asked if the property purchased appeared to be an important part of the employer's own commercial premises, and thus potentially difficult to realise . . .

The SFO are clearly concerned that the scheme should not be abused and used for the member's benefit. They will not normally give permission for the following type of investments: villa in Spain; yacht on the French Riviera; works of art; certain UK residential property; woodlands leased back to the member.

Hybrid Schemes

The Hybrid scheme is a combination of the self-administered and the managed arrangement. It requires that an annual premium is paid into an insured contract, which may be on a with-profit or unit-linked basis, and any further contributions can form part of the self-administered fund. Loan-back facilities are normally available.

Insurance companies will take on the schemes' administration but will make charges based upon the premium which is part of the insured contract. The Hybrid scheme is often appropriate for those who want self-administration but are not yet in a position to pay contributions at a sufficiently high level and are concerned about the costs of a fully Self-administered scheme. In this way the annual contribution to the insured fund can, depending on each insurance company's terms, remain at the level when the scheme is set up with any future increases being made into the self-administered fund. The contributions to the insured fund should be at a relatively low level if self-administration is what you are really looking for so that the charges are kept reasonably low.

Executive 'Top Hat' Schemes

The 1986/87 Directors Rewards survey, published by the Institute of Directors and Rewards Regional Surveys Ltd, revealed that 84 per cent of directors (excluding the managing director or chairman) were in the basic Company pension scheme and the average company contribution was nearly £6,000 per annum. This is much higher than the average level of pension contribution which is paid for an employee.

When forming a Company pension scheme, the directors may wish to distinguish between the key personnel and the employees. They may feel that for most employees the proposed pension scheme will be adequate but they may wish to provide extra benefits for the executives. 'Top hat' schemes have increased in popularity with approximately 43 per cent more executives joining such schemes between 1980 and 1985. However, in the mid-1980s, only 25 per cent of executives were in 'top hat' schemes. It could be contentious to provide higher benefits for some employees within one scheme and so it is often decided to set up a separate executive scheme which provides additional benefits.

Executive pension schemes which are approved under section 19 Finance Act 1970 provide the following benefits:

(a) a pension of up to 1/60 final salary for each year of service;
(b) a reduced pension and a tax-free lump sum not exceeding 3/80 of final salary for each year of service;
(c) the above benefits are to be taken at a pre-selected pension date of 60 to 70 for males and 55 to 70 for females;
(d) no Death-in-service benefits may be provided.

However, discretionary approval under section 20 Finance Act 1970 may be given for a more flexible scheme which may include the following features:

(a) additional maximum benefits for those who will have less than 40 years of service; or
(b) pensions for widows on Death-in-service or children or dependants; or
(c) Death-in-service benefits of up to four times the employee's final remuneration; or
(d) benefits payable on retirement before the specified age; or
(e) a return of contributions under certain circumstances.

The great majority of pension schemes are approved under section 20 Finance Act 1970 and their initial and continued approval is, therefore, subject to the Inland Revenue's discretionary powers.

Executive 'top hat' schemes are often run alongside the main scheme and provide for greater benefits which can be received after a shorter service period, as many executives are recruited mid-career and few will have served a company for 40 years by the time they retire.

Administration savings can be made by identifying the benefits for the executives and specifying these in an 'exchange letter' which is issued in duplicate and acknowledged by the member. A trust will then be formed for the purpose of the scheme. This is the simplest way of forming the trust. However the trust is established, the benefits will be governed by Inland Revenue limits. In this way the executive will have a more readily identifiable fund and the additional benefits for the executive can be provided through the Executive 'top hat' pension scheme outside the rules of the staff scheme.

Loan-Backs

One of the attractive features of Occupational schemes is that the pension scheme can make loans to the company. Interest must be paid at a commercial rate which, like the contribution, is tax deductible to the company and is received tax-free by the pension scheme. This facility can help a company if it experiences liquidity problems and can encourage directors to fund pension schemes as illustrated from the following cash flow projection. Although a small Self-administered scheme cannot normally lend more than 50 per cent of the fund to the company, there are no specific restrictions of this nature for other company schemes.

Occupational Pension Schemes

Table 8.5

	£
Payment into pension scheme	100,000
Corporation tax relief at (say) 35 per cent	(35,000)
	65,000
Loan-back from pension scheme	(50,000)
Permanent loss of cash	15,000
Annual interest payable £50,000 at (say) 12 per cent	6,000

The Inland Revenue is tightening up on the availability of such loans from small Self-administered schemes which are only permitted if it can be shown that they are provided for a specific commercial purpose. If these loans are set up for a term of less than one year, no tax needs to be deducted from the interest payments; if the loans are for one year, or longer, tax needs to be deducted at source from the interest payments and paid to the Inland Revenue.

Chapter 9
Additional Voluntary Contributions

If you are in an Occupational pension scheme, the level of contributions to the scheme, or the benefits to be provided under the scheme, will be set by its rules. It may, for example, under a Money purchase scheme, require the company to contribute 8 per cent of your salary if you pay 4 per cent. Those employees who are conscious of the need for retirement planning may want to 'top-up' their scheme as it is unlikely it will be generally providing the maximum permissible benefits. If the scheme rules allow you to 'top-up' the scheme's benefits then you can do so by making an additional voluntary contribution ('AVC') into the scheme. From 6 April 1988, the scheme will have to allow an AVC arrangement but the trustees can decide how the money is invested. Alternatively, from October 1987 employees can pay AVCs into a 'free-standing' scheme which is independent of the company's pension scheme. The maximum allowable AVC which an employee can pay is 15 per cent of his salary after deducting any payment he is already making under the scheme. The 15 per cent limit is not restricted by contributions which are made by the employer but is subject to the overall Inland Revenue limits and the special rules which apply to simplified Money purchase schemes.

The limits in Table 9.1 are not the only restriction to the amount which can be paid into an AVC scheme. The pension benefits from the Company scheme and those produced by the AVC arrangement cannot exceed the Inland Revenue's maximum of two-thirds final salary. This

Table 9.1
A woman earning £15,000 is a member of a pension scheme under which the company pays 8 per cent of her salary and she pays 4 per cent. The maximum AVC is as follows.

	% of salary	£
Company	8	1,200
Employee — scheme payment	4	600
AVC	11	1,650
	15	2,250
Total payments	23	3,450

is an added complication as those advising on the AVC payment which can be made will need to take account of the benefits from the main scheme, except in the case of the simplified Money purchase arrangement. This may require advice from the scheme's actuary to avoid over-funding. This problem could be avoided if the Government were to change the rules in the future so that the Inland Revenue limits were not to apply to AVC arrangements, in which case the limit would be on contributions only (such as the PPS) and not contributions and benefits.

It is interesting to note that the legislation refers to '. . . 15 per cent or such higher percentage as the Board may in a particular case prescribe, of his remuneration for that year'. It is understood that the 15 per cent limit can only be exceeded in very special circumstances. For example, if the employee pays an amount on a regular basis and misses a year, the Board may exercise their discretion and allow a late payment but not so that the total payments made in the employment period exceed 15 per cent of earnings.

Tax Benefits

The existing AVC attracts the same tax benefits which are associated with pension schemes generally (but new AVCs will not attract the tax-free cash sum) as set out below:

1. The contribution attracts income tax relief at the member's top marginal rates.
2. The AVC fund grows entirely tax-free.
3. The fund may produce tax-free cash if it was set up before 8 April 1987.

The effect of those benefits is illustrated below.

Table 9.2

A man who is five years from retirement is considering paying £1,000 per annum into an investment plan. His top marginal income tax rate is 50 per cent and it is assumed that either fund will grow at 12 per cent gross per annum. Any higher-rate tax will be taken from the fund.

	AVC plan	Building society deposit
	£	£
Gross annual payment	2,000	1,000
Tax relief at (say) 50 per cent	(1,000)	–
Net cost to individual	1,000	1,000
Accumulated fund after five years	14,230	5,975

Problem areas

The ability to pay AVCs has depended upon the pension scheme rules in the past. Many employees would like to have taken advantage of the AVC arrangement but could not do so because of the way in which the scheme rules were written. It is understood that only about 10 per cent of scheme members have AVC arrangements. As they cannot take out a retirement annuity while in pensionable employment, they were unable to 'top-up' their scheme.

This problem has now been overcome. With effect from October 1987 an employee can set up his own Free-standing AVC arrangement. As a Free-standing arrangement, the AVC fund is outside the main fund and can be separately identified and transferred when he changes job. A member can, if he wishes, use a different investment house from that of the group pension fund. However, it is likely to be more expensive as it will be costed on an individual rather than a group basis.

The normal retirement date of the Free-standing AVC will be governed by the rules relating to the main scheme. However, if the employee changes job, the retirement date can then be linked to that of his new employer's scheme which could be earlier or later. The main scheme rules may require amendment to take account of the Free-standing AVC as, for example, the maximum benefits from the main scheme will need to take account of those under the Free-standing arrangement.

The other main obstacle to an employee 'topping-up' his pension was that by making an AVC he was committing himself to further payments. This is because the SFO stated in their Practice Notices that:

> 'Payments once begun should be terminated only if the member's circumstances have so changed since he started making voluntary contributions that to continue paying them would involve him in financial hardship. But in practice if there is an understanding that, barring such unforeseen circumstances, the member will continue to make them on a uniform basis for not less than five years (or until retirement if that is earlier) they may be allowed as ordinary annual contributions.'

A member may have had surplus funds this year but could not guarantee that these funds would be available next year. For example, an increase in school fees, mortgage

Additional Voluntary Contributions

interest rates, tax rates, etc, would reduce his capacity to pay.

This problem has been overcome as a member may, subject to the scheme's rules permitting, make a 'one-off' AVC with effect from 6 April 1987. Therefore, he can make a payment one year and decide whether or not he wishes to pay an AVC again next year and, if so, at what level. If a person wishes to 'top-up' his pension arrangements then (subject to Inland Revenue limits) he should now be able to do so. A summary of this is below:

1. If you are self-employed or not in a pension scheme — this can be done by the Retirement annuity or Personal pension scheme contract.
2. If you are in an Occupational pension scheme — this can be done by the AVC.
3. If you are a controlling director — you may wish to arrange for the company rather than you to 'top-up' your benefits.

Tax-free Cash

While the above proposals are welcomed, so that it will be easier for employees to make personal contributions, the new AVC arrangements will no longer be able to produce a tax-free lump sum. The new no commutation rule will apply to new schemes and members joining existing schemes. It is understood that it will not apply to AVC arrangements which were in force before 8 April 1987 even if they are improved after that date. The Government believes that the AVC 'top-up' should be used to maximise pension benefits but not the cash element. This is one of the anti-avoidance measures which have been introduced.

The AVC schemes which were set up before 8 April 1987 will be unaffected so that the AVC payments will continue to build up a fund which can create tax-free cash. However, AVC arrangements formed after 7 April 1987 will no longer do so.

The new rules, which prevent an AVC from producing tax-free cash, will not only affect pension-linked mortgages, they could also be an obstacle to job mobility. For example, if an employee is currently in an AVC scheme which provides tax-free cash and wishes to move job, he will join a company which will need to set up a new AVC arrangement for him. Therefore, if he stays at his present job, any future AVC payment to the existing scheme can produce tax-free cash whereas if he moves, future AVC payments to the arrangement with his new employer will not. This disparity is unfortunate as it acts against freedom of movement which is said to be one of the main aims of the Government. However, in practice job mobility may not be such a problem as the tax-free cash which may be taken from an Occupational scheme must be cut back by any cash which is taken from the AVC arrangement.

An AVC arrangement may be more attractive than a salary sacrifice. The latter arrangement involves the employee taking a drop in salary so that the company will agree to 'top-up' a scheme with the amount saved from the salary reduction. The AVC arrangement will not involve a reduction in salary levels upon which pension benefits will be calculated but new AVC arangements can no longer produce tax-free cash. Also, a salary sacrifice will produce savings in national insurance contributions.

Future Contributions

The new Free-standing AVC arrangements will be available from October 1987 so that employees will be able to use the investment house of their choice.

Even though tax-free cash will no longer be available from new schemes, the removal of the shackles which

Additional Voluntary Contributions

previously existed will enable millions of employees in Company schemes with gaps in their membership or a poor history of contributions to 'top-up' their pension benefits in a way in which they can control and understand. This will be a target for the direct sales force of finance houses and so professional advice will be needed to ensure that the plan fully takes account of their wishes.

The AVC arrangement has often been used by those nearing retirement but it should be adopted by any employee who has spare cash to invest. The AVC is to be paid after deduction of basic-rate tax, like mortgage interest under the MIRAS system. The basic rate of tax will be claimed from the Inland Revenue by the scheme administrators. Any higher-rate relief will be claimable by the member. It should be included in the notice of coding so that the tax relief is received when the salary is paid rather than having to wait for a tax repayment following submission of the tax return for the relevant year.

Chapter 10
Maximum Funding

The pension scheme can provide a variety of benefits, many of which are often unappreciated and therefore not adequately provided for by the scheme. The funding levels of an Occupational pension scheme will depend upon the range and level of benefits which are to be provided. They cannot exceed the maximum levels which are set by the Inland Revenue and which will be considered in greater detail later in this chapter. As the benefits are limited, the funding levels are also bound by the same constraints.

Unlike Occupational pension schemes, retirement annuity schemes, the new PPS and Simplified Money

Table 10.1

Type of scheme	Explicit restriction on contribution	Explicit restriction on benefits
Group 1		
Occupational pension schemes, (excluding new simplified Money purchase and AVCs) and 'top hat' schemes.	No	Yes
Group 2		
Retirement annuities, Personal pension schemes, new simplified Money purchase scheme.	Yes	No
Group 3		
AVC arrangements	Yes	Yes

purchase schemes have contribution levels which are a percentage of earnings but have no limit of the level of pension which is produced. Therefore instead of having the limit on the level of pension which the fund can produce which, in turn, governs the contribution level, there is no limit on the values of the fund but only a limit on the money which can be invested each year. The position can be summarised as in Table 10.1.

Funding for a Pension

The maximum funding level of the group 2 arrangements is 17.5 per cent of earnings, unless you are over 50 in which case the contribution may be paid at a higher level. Occupational pension schemes are governed by the Inland Revenue limits on the pension which can be taken from the fund. The maximum pension is normally expressed as two-thirds of final remuneration at retirement, but this definition needs to be examined in more detail to understand how it is calculated.

The maximum proportion of two-thirds depends upon the number of years the director or employee has served the company. For members who joined a pension scheme before 17 March 1987, it is possible to take the maximum pension of two-thirds final salary if only 10 years have been served at normal retirement date, otherwise the pension entitlement will be scaled down. For those members who join a scheme after 16 March 1987, 20 years must be served otherwise the benefit will be scaled down.

This change was to prevent privileged directors and employees taking maximum benefits after a relatively short period of time. The maximum proportion of final salary is set out in Appendix 10. The percentages set out here are the maximum proportions of final remuneration which can be taken if a director or employee has not served 40 years with

Maximum Funding

Table 10.2

A man retires at 60 with final remuneration of £30,000. He joined the company when he was 45.

	If he joined the scheme before 17 March 1987	If he joined the scheme after 16 March 1987
	£	£
Maximum pension per annum	20,000	15,000

the company before normal retirement date. These are uplifted scales which apply to employees as the maximum of two-thirds final remuneration will, for most employees, only be received after 40 years of service. This is because most pension schemes use a fraction of 1/60 of final salary for each year of service. The more basic schemes work on a fraction of 1/80. Some very good schemes work on a fraction of 1/45 so that the maximum pension entitlement can be reached after only 30 years of service. Obviously, a scheme providing benefits based on 1/45 of final salary will need a much greater funding level than one based on 1/80 of final salary, but it will have the benefit to the employer of making

Table 10.3

An employee retires on final remuneration of £20,000 after having served 20 years with the company. The annuity rate is assumed to be 12 per cent.

	Fraction of final salary		
	1/45	1/60	1/80
	£	£	£
Pension entitlement per annum	8,889	6,667	5,000
Fund required	74,074	55,555	41,667

valuable employees who have served many years with the company less likely to leave as they would normally be jeopardising their pension rights by doing so. The benefit to the employee can be seen from the previous illustration.

The final remuneration is normally taken to be the average annual remuneration of the last three years of service.

Table 10.4

An employee retires on a maximum pension of 2/3 final remuneration. The final remuneration calculation ignores the effects of dynamisation.

	£
Remuneration — year of retirement	30,000
Remuneration — penultimate year	27,000
Remuneration — pre-penultimate year	24,000
	81,000
Final remuneration £81,000 ÷ 3	27,000
Pension £27,000 × 2/3	18,000

The term final remuneration no longer includes amounts assessable under income tax Schedule E under certain provisions governing share option and share incentive arrangements, and under the provisions relating to payments on termination or variation of employment. This is so that pension benefits can no longer be artificially inflated by creating a tax charge in the above circumstances. The changes will apply to the acquisition of shares (or of the right to acquire them), the appropriation of shares and the granting of options on or after 17 March 1987.

Under the Inland Revenue's discretionary powers, two alternative definitions may be approved for the calculation of final benefits:

Maximum Funding

(a) for any single year in the last five before retirement; basic salary plus fluctuating emoluments (which may have to be averaged over a three-year period), such as bonuses, commission, the taxable value of benefits in kind etc; or

(b) average total emoluments for any period of 3 or more years ending in the last 10 before retirement (this can enable a scheme member to use the 13 years before retirement). This average can be increased by dynamisation which is considered further on in the text.

These definitions have often been used for executive 'top hat' schemes, to maximise benefits for privileged employees. Controlling directors (ie directors who own, or control, 20 per cent or more of the company's ordinary share capital) cannot use method (a). These rules could be abused for controlling directors by taking a large pay increase in the final year or resigning from the Board of Directors shortly before retirement. In an attempt to avoid this abuse for those retiring after 17 March 1987 the following changes have been made:

1. If the employee has been a controlling director within 10 years before retirement or if annual 'final remuneration' is £100,000 or more in 1987/88 and subsequent years then method (b) above only must be used.

2. If an employee has annual 'final remuneration' of £100,000 or more and retires before 6 April 1991, the relevant annual remuneration can be based on method (a) above, provided the pension calculation is based on the 1986/87 salary.

In both cases, the present rule permitting dynamisation of the figure for 'final remuneration' will continue to apply.

These provisions should still not prevent controlling directors from artificially increasing pension benefits by maximising remuneration for three years before retirement.

Table 10.5

A controlling director retires at age 60. It is assumed that annuity rates of 12 per cent are appropriate.

	Maximum pension £	Fund required £
Average remuneration of £30,000 per annum	20,000	166,667
Uplifted remuneration		
Average remuneration three years before retirement — £60,000	40,000	333,334
Additional remuneration £30,000 × three	£90,000	
Requires an uplift in the pension fund of	£166,667	

The Chancellor's broad intention is that employees who were in service and members of a scheme before 17 March 1987 and who remain with the same employer or who effectively remain members of the same scheme, should not be adversely affected by the proposed changes. In general, the situations which are set out in Appendix 11 will not normally be regarded as being caught by the above changes.

Dynamisation

Where final remuneration includes a year which is more than 12 months before normal retirement date the relevant income figures may be adjusted in line with the movement in the RPI to the date of determination. This is called dynamisation and it can substantially increase the level of benefits.

It is not possible to use a dynamised final remuneration to increase the percentage of total benefits which are

Table 10.6

	Actual remuneration £	Increase in RPI %	Dynamised remuneration £
Salary of 12 months before retirement	30,000	n/a	30,000
Penultimate year	29,000	10	31,900
Pre-penultimate year	28,000	8	33,264
	87,000	–	95,164
Final remuneration £87,000 ÷ 3	29,000	–	–
Dynamised final remuneration £95,164 ÷ 3			31,721

available in the form of tax-free cash alone. Dynamisation may only be used where the fund available to purchase benefits is larger than that required to purchase maximum pension benefits based on actual final remuneration. Therefore, dynamisation can increase funding levels to uplift both the tax-free lump sum and the residual pension by equal proportions.

Maximum pension

As mentioned above, the funding level of an Occupational pension scheme is restricted by the maximum pension which can be taken at retirement. The company's annual contribution can either be made on a flat-rate basis (which is typical for small pension schemes) or at a level which will escalate in line with members' earnings (which is typical in

Group pension schemes). A Money purchase scheme will normally be funded by the employer and employee as a percentage of the payroll so that the annual contribution can be determined each year. The Money purchase scheme will only be as good as the contributions that go into it and their subsequent management. The funding of a Final salary scheme will depend upon the advice from an actuary as to the amount to be contributed to ensure that the fund can pay out the necessary benefits. The level of contributions to produce maximum benefits for older members is high. The benefits produced by the fund are discounted at 5 per cent per annum to produce a more realistic picture and the detailed workings in respect of the following illustration are set out in Appendix 12.

Table 10.7

A man aged 45 on a salary of £30,000 will retire at age 65. His salary is projected to grow at 5 per cent per annum and the fund at 10 per cent per annum.

	£	Benefits discounted at 5% per annum £
Projected salary on retirement	79,599	30,000
Maximum pension of 2/3 guaranteed five years	53,066	20,000
Fund required using an annuity rate of 12.3 per cent	430,236	
Annual contribution escalating at 5 per cent per annum required — 16 per cent per annum of salary (ie £4,800 increasing to £12,129)		

Maximum Funding

Often the salary increases will exceed 5 per cent per annum so that the above funding rate of 16 per cent would be too low to produce a two-thirds pension on retirement. A funding rate of nearer 20 per cent may be more appropriate. Many employers and employees in Money purchase schemes are not funding at this level so that there would be considerable scope to 'top-up' the scheme before considering additional benefits which could be provided.

Funding levels will normally take into account a projected growth rate of the pension fund. The rate must be reasonable in the light of long-term trends and its relationship to inflation and salary increases. The maximum funding of a Personal pension scheme or Retirement annuity arrangement will not depend upon the resulting final salary, but rather on the amount which can be paid in (ie 17.5 per cent of earnings increasing with higher percentages after 50 years of age). The benefits taken out of the scheme depend upon how much is invested and the investment performance of the fund.

Inflation

Funding for a pension based on two-thirds of final salary may appear to produce an adequate income stream, if expenses fall by one-third after retirement. However, inflation can quickly erode the value of the pension. During the 1980s we have become accustomed to inflation of around 5 per cent but since the rate of inflation reached almost 25 per cent in the 1970s it would be prudent, if at all possible, to fund for an Index-linked pension. If you will not be receiving a maximum pension at retirement then you could use your accumulated fund in a Money purchase scheme to take either a higher Flat-rate pension or a lower pension which increases each year. The escalating pension will start at a lower figure but will overtake the Flat-rate pension in time.

For example, a member who could take a Flat-rate pension of, say, £24,000 per annum may prefer to take a pension which escalates at 5 per cent per annum. It will start at approximately £17,000, reach £25,000 after eight years and exceed the Flat-rate pension thereafter.

The Inland Revenue will allow you to fund for a pension based on two-thirds of final remuneration which escalates at up to the RPI to counter the effects of inflation. If you are able to influence the pension benefits which will be received you may wish to fund for a pension which is likely to be inflation proof.

Table 10.8

Facts as in the previous example, except that the company wishes to fund for a pension based on 2/3 final salary with the pension escalating at 5 per cent per annum.

	Original funding £	Revised funding £	Increase £
Fund required	430,000	598,000	168,000
Contribution increasing at 5 per cent per annum	4,800	6,700	1,900
Contribution as percentage of salary	16%	22%	6%

Widow's Pension

When planning for retirement it is important to consider not only your income requirement but also that of your spouse after you die. If as a married couple, you and your wife are able to live off your pension when you retire then on your death the income requirement should not be as great, as your annual expenses will no longer be incurred. As a 'rule of thumb' approach, your widow may be able to manage on two-thirds of your pension and this is the maximum Widow's pension that the Inland Revenue will allow. Therefore, you could fund not only for your pension based on two-thirds of final salary but, in addition, a widow's pension based on four-ninths of final salary (ie two-thirds of your pension). While an important benefit, its provision will increase the level of funding required.

Table 10.9

Facts in the previous example except that the company wishes to fund not only for a pension based on 2/3 final salary escalating at 5 per cent per annum, but also a Widow's pension of 4/9 final salary which also escalates at 5 per cent per annum.

	Previous funding £	Revised funding £	Increase £
Fund required	598,000	726,000	128,000
Contribution increasing at 5 per cent per annum	6,700	8,100	1,400
Contribution as percentage of salary	22%	27%	5%

A Widow's pension may continue for life but if the scheme provides for a pension for a child then this must cease when the child ceases to be a dependant (normally on reaching 18 or, if later, on ceasing full-time education). In addition, an employee may surrender part of his own pension to provide further benefits for his wife and dependants. The Dependants' pension must not exceed his own.

The Personal pension scheme can fund for a widow's (or widower's) pension. A retirement annuity cannot specifically provide a Widow's pension although at retirement the fund can be used to buy a pension for you together with a Widow's pension.

As you will see there are numerous benefits which can be provided by the pension scheme as illustrated in the following table.

Table 10.10

A man aged 45 on a current salary of £30,000 which is likely to escalate at 5 per cent per annum until he retires at age 65. It is assumed the fund will grow at 10 per cent per annum. The funding required to provide the following benefits is set out below.

Benefit provided	Required fund £	Annual cost increasing at 5% £	Cost as % of current salary %
Maximum pension of 2/3 of final remuneration	430,000	4,800	16
Pension increasing at 5 per cent per annum	168,000	1,900	6
	598,000	6,700	22
Widow's pension in retirement 4/9 of final remuneration escalating at 5 per cent per annum	128,000	1,400	5
	726,000	8,100	27

You should consider the range and level of benefits which you need as an employee and those which as an employer you may wish to provide. The above example has been produced as *an illustration only* and can only be used as a guide. However, if you are looking for maximum benefits you may need to 'top-up' your scheme by an AVC arrangement which can now be made on a one-off basis.

Table 10.11

Facts as per the above example, but the contributions are currently as follows.

	% of salary
Employer	8
Employee	4
	12
Contributions needed to maximise benefits	15
	27

Life Assurance

The question which needs to be asked is, 'If I die tomorrow will my family be able to maintain our current standard of living?' If the answer is 'no' and, in particular, if the family's income will be dramatically reduced, then some form of life assurance protection will be necessary. Consider the example in Table 10.12.

The pension scheme is one of the most effective methods of providing life assurance protection. The Inland Revenue allow Occupational schemes to pay four times the final remuneration before death as a lump sum payment to the scheme's beneficiaries, usually those who have been nominated by the member. It may be necessary for the fund to take out life assurance until the member's fund exceeds four times his salary, or the fund may wish to provide separately for the Death-in-service benefits so that the remaining pension benefits are unaffected. The cost to the pension fund to provide the Death-in-service cover may not be large.

The Daily Telegraph Pensions Guide

Table 10.12

An individual is 40 years of age and married with two young children. He is an employee earning £30,000 per annum, and his wife does not work. His assets are a house worth £100,000 (on which there is a £30,000 endowment-linked mortgage) and investments of £10,000. The expenditure would fall by £5,000 upon his death.

Net spendable income		*Current position*	*Position after death*
	£	£	£
Salary	–	30,000	
Gross income from investments, approx.	–	1,000	1,000
		31,000	
Mortgage interest payment, approx.	–	(3,600)	
		27,400	–
Endowment policy payments, approx.	(400)	–	–
Income tax	(7,275)	–	–
		(7,675)	–
		19,725	–
Expenditure, approx.		(17,000)	(12,000)
Net surplus/(deficit)		2,725	(11,000)

Table 10.13

A woman aged 30 is on a salary of £30,000 per annum.

Death-in-service cover of £30,000 × 4   £120,000

Level term assurance for (say) seven years (say) £160 per annum

Maximum Funding

The Death-in-service cover would improve the position as follows.

Table 10.14.

		Position after death	
		With DIS cover	Without DIS cover
	£	£ per annum	£ per annum
Cash from Death-in-service cover	120,000	–	–
Investment income £130,000/10,000 × (say) 10 per cent		13,000	1,000
Income tax		(2,485)	–
		10,515	1,000
Expenditure		(12,000)	(12,000)
Net deficit		(1,485)	(11,000)

As is evident, the Death-in-service cover will go some way towards meeting the family's needs, but a Death-in-service pension may also be required as described on the following page. The Death-in-service protection will normally be paid to the wife. However, if the wife is already well protected, inheritance tax savings can be achieved by making the lump sum payment directly to other beneficiaries, such as the children. This is because the payment can be made without paying inheritance tax, whereas if it is paid to the wife it will form part of her estate therefore aggravating the inheritance tax position on her death.

The PPS provides for a contribution to produce a Death-in-service payment which, like the retirement annuity rules, is up to 5 per cent of the net relevant earnings. There is no ceiling on the lump sum payment as it will be governed by the premium which is paid to provide the cover. The lump sum can then be used to buy a pension for life.

Table 10.15

The final remuneration of an individual is £50,000. If he dies in service and the pension fund has £200,000 this can be paid to his spouse (whose wealth will exceed £330,000) or children.

	£
Payment to spouse	200,000
Potential inheritance tax on death of spouse at (say) 60 per cent	(120,000)
	80,000
Payment direct to children without inheritance tax	200,000
Saving	120,000

Death-in-service Pension

The pension scheme can fund for not only a lump sum which will be paid on Death-in-service, but also a pension payable to the widow, as the normal Widow's pension will only be payable following the death of member in retirement. The earlier example showed that income from a lump sum payment of £120,000 will reduce the deficiency, but this may not be sufficient. The fund required to produce Death-in-service pension cover for the widow in addition to Death-in-retirement cover may not be high.

Salary Sacrifice

This arrangement involves the employee voluntarily taking a lower salary so that the employer can use the reduction to fund for pension benefits. An employer may be willing to set up a scheme for employees if they take a salary sacrifice so that the remuneration package is not increased. This arrangement may be useful if a member wants to contribute more than 15 per cent of his earnings.

Table 10.16

An employee earns £20,000 per annum and wants to contribute £4,500 to her employer's scheme.

No salary sacrifice	£
Maximum contribution £20,000 × 15 per cent	3,000
Shortfall	1,500
	4,500
Salary sacrifice of £1,765	
Paid by company	1,765
Maximum contribution (£20,000 − 1,765) × 15 per cent	2,735
	4,500

The disadvantages of a salary sacrifice are as follows:

(a) it may reduce the 'final remuneration' upon which the pension and tax-free cash may be based;
(b) the lump sum Death-in-service payment may include a refund of contributions which the member has made and this will not include the salary sacrifice;
(c) if a member leaves a scheme, it may, in certain circumstances, refund members' contributions but, again, this will not include salary sacrifices.

The employer will benefit from reduced national insurance charges as a salary attracts national insurance while a pension contribution does not.

Over-funding

The tax benefits of pension schemes have encouraged many controlling directors to maximise their pension schemes. The strong performance of the UK stock market has produced large investment gains within funds which may not have been anticipated when the contribution was made. Also, many members of pension schemes have been retired early because of redundancy. These factors have contributed to certain Final salary pension schemes being over-funded. In some cases the pension fund has grown so large that its value may have exceeded that of its company. These cash-rich companies are very attractive to their competitors for potential take-overs. In order to curtail this, the Finance Act 1986 contains provisions to regulate pension scheme surpluses. These provisions do not apply to small Self-administered schemes and insured schemes under which no valuation report is required. For the purpose of the legislation, surpluses will be calculated on a specific and more stringent Government basis than is usually used in practice. The following action *must* be taken if these calculations produce a surplus:

(a) the employer may enjoy a contribution holiday for a defined period of up to five years; or
(b) the scheme can improve the benefits up to the Inland Revenue limits so that the surplus funds are released for that purpose (eg to index-link the pension); or
(c) the scheme must repay the surplus to the employer.

Any combination of the above alternatives may be used to eliminate the surplus. The last option is likely to be the least palatable. As tax relief is received on the payment to the scheme, the repayment will attract a tax charge at the rate of 40 per cent. Other reliefs, such as trading losses, cannot be used to reduce the tax charge.

A *de-minimus* limit exists so that the above conditions will not apply if the pension scheme is over-funded by less than 5 per cent. (If the fund's surplus on a defined basis as specified by the Government is more than 5 per cent of the value of the scheme's liability then this *de-minimus* limit will not apply.) Recently over-funded pension schemes have been a target in take-over bids as the new owner can then insist that the surplus is repaid out of the fund, even though it is taxable. It is important to ensure that the scheme is not over-funded if you are selling a business as you could find that your pension scheme will need to repay funds to the company which may no longer be owned by you. If the scheme is over-funded it is important for a seller to allow for this in the purchase price.

Spreading of Relief

Corporation tax relief will be available in respect of employers' contributions to pension schemes in the year of payment so long as the pension payment is a regular contribution. To be regarded as a regular contribution, payments must be maintained and there must usually be at least three annual payments. A single contribution will normally attract tax relief but this may be spread over up to five years if it exceeds the regular contribution (or £10,000 if more).

Chapter 11
Job Mobility

A pension used to be regarded as a reward for long service and loyalty to the company. Consequently, many companies were reluctant to reward leavers with their maximum pension entitlement if they were leaving, especially if they were going to work for a competitor. The position was aggravated if the company operated a Group scheme because any payment made from the scheme to the leaver reduced the funds available to those remaining in employment. This could happen when a scheme was poorly funded.

One of the major problems which has yet to be overcome is the poor deal which an employee may receive when he changes jobs. During the recent Parliamentary debates Sir Brandon Rhys Williams announced that in 1986 it was estimated that early leavers are losing £1,000 million per annum because of the way in which their transfer values are calculated. Many ministers have wrestled with this problem over the past two decades. In 1969, Richard Crossman recognised the need to protect an employee's pension rights. The Social Security Act 1973 also tackled the problem, while further improvements were made in the Finance Act 1981 and the Social Security Act 1985. But none of these attempts has found a completely satisfactory solution. So, a man who leaves his job in mid-career is likely to be in a worse position than someone who remains with one company throughout, even though one-job employees are relatively rare.

The options which are open to employers and scheme

administrators depend upon the rules of the pension scheme and any overriding pensions legislation. Over the years many companies have changed the rules so that the leaver can get a better deal, but others still provide for the minimum benefits required under the legislation.

Scheme administrators have been reluctant to accept benefits transferred by the new employee from his old scheme if they were restricted, as it may result in the new employer taking on an additional burden if he is funding for the employee's previous working life without a fair transfer. This is a problem which has still not been fully addressed.

Transfers Between Occupational Schemes

Employees who are members of an Occupational pension scheme have three options open to them when they leave employment:

(a) leave the benefits in the current pension scheme; or
(b) transfer the benefits to the new employer's scheme; or
(c) transfer the benefits to a 'Section 32 Buy-Out' policy.

The first option has been required since 1975 while the other alternatives have only been required in recent years. The calculation of the Deferred pension is more generous now and professional guidelines have been published regarding transfer values. Since the passing of the Social Security Act 1973, which took effect from April 1975, accrued benefits must be preserved for a leaver if he has completed five years' membership of the scheme. The benefits which must be preserved under the Social Security Act 1973 include the following:

(a) a Personal pension at normal retirement date;

(b) the tax-free cash sum at normal retirement date if the benefits are provided at normal retirement date;
(c) a Widow's pension payable in retirement.

They do not include a Death-before-retirement payment.

The calculation of leaving service benefits under a final salary scheme is now very complicated. The first step is to calculate the member's deferred pension. If the scheme is contracted-out, then the GMP must be protected. (The DHSS regulations widen the scope for the transfer of GMPs in two ways. They allow the transfer of GMPs to and from schemes which, although no longer contracted out, are still subject to the financial supervision of the Occupational Pensions Board. This may help members of schemes in

---

Table 11.1

A man aged 45 leaves his job on a salary of £12,000. He has 20 years of service and will retire at 65 on £31,840. His salary grows at 5 per cent per annum in line with inflation during the period. His new employer operates a similar scheme which provides for a pension based on 1/60 for each year served.

	No escalation from first employer	Full escalation from employer
	£ per annum	£ per annum
Pension from existing scheme £12,000 × 20/60	4,000	10,614
Pension from new employer £31,840 × 20/60	10,614	10,614
Pension at retirement	14,614	21,228
Pension if he remains in one employment throughout £31,840 × 40/60	21,228	21,228
Loss of pension by moving	6,614	nil

respect of companies which are merging or in take-overs. Secondly, they allow GMPs which have been bought out through an insurance policy or annuity contract to be transferred subsequently to a contracted-out scheme, or one under the financial supervision of the Occupational Pensions Board.)

If an employee is in a Final salary scheme then the benefit will be based upon his salary when leaving the scheme. Some schemes allow for some form of index-linking of the salary while others do not. Clearly, if no account is taken for inflation and future salary increases, the pension from the existing scheme will be greatly eroded as shown above.

At present, escalation must be given for the proportion of the pension (in excess of the GMP) which accrues after 1 January 1985 so that employees may find themselves between the above two extremes, if only part of the pension for the previous employer's scheme escalates. However, as the post-1985 period increases, the proportion of the deferred pension which must be escalated will increase until eventually all deferred pensions will be subject to escalation. If an employee is in a Money purchase scheme which entitles him to the benefits provided by the assets for him if he stays in service until normal retirement date, it should be possible to value the accumulated fund when he leaves. Clearly, it will be smaller than if he had stayed until retirement as fewer premiums would have been paid and the growth of the fund will only be taken until he leaves, possibly after taking account of charges. Employers will generally be seeking to provide the best deal for those remaining rather than for the leavers. If the scheme is improved by, for example, reducing the number of years of service before maximum benefits are received, it is unlikely that this will apply to any members who have remained in the scheme but have left the employment.

In order to protect the finances of existing Occupational

schemes, the DHSS regulations provide that, unless the scheme's rules allow, an employee who leaves the scheme without leaving his job will not have the right to a transfer value of the benefits he or she has built up before the new PPS arrangements start.

Post-1985 Service

The Social Security Act 1985 has gone some way to improving the position for so-called 'early leavers'. For members of Final salary schemes who leave service on or after 1 January 1986, the Deferred pensions must be revalued up to normal retirement date in line with the RPI or at 5 per cent per annum compound whichever is the less. As explained above, the pension to be revalued is that relating to post-1 January 1985 service. A growth of up to 5 per cent per annum is unlikely to keep pace with future salary rises over a long period of time so that the leaver is still likely to lose out, in pension terms, but by much less

---

Table 11.2

A man aged 40 leaves his job on 1 January 1988 on a salary of £12,000. He has 20 years of service and will retire at 60 on £31,840. His salary grows at 5 per cent per annum and his new employer operates a similar scheme which produces a pension based on 1/60 for each year service.

	£	£
Deferred pension on leaving say £12,000 × 20/60	–	4,000
Pre-1 January 1985 service £4,000 × 17/20	–	3,400
Post-1 January 1985 service £4,000 × 3/20	600	–
Post-1 January 1985 service revalued at 5 per cent per annum		1,592
		4,992

than before. Money purchase schemes will be required to increase early leavers' benefits in the same way as if they had remained in pensionable service. Table 11.2 shows why the Social Security Act 1985 does not go far enough.

Rather than leave the benefits in the employee's old pension scheme he may wish to transfer the benefits to his new employer's Occupational pension scheme. Although he has a legal right to a transfer value there is no legal obligation on the new scheme to accept the transfer payment. Also, if the employee is likely to suffer in leaving his last employment, he may be reluctant to transfer his benefits to another scheme in case he suffers again from a future career move.

Section 32 Policies

An increasingly popular option now for employees who change jobs is to transfer their benefits to a 'Section 32 Buy-Out Policy'. It results in the transfer value being paid from the scheme, in respect of the employee's accrued benefits, to a single premium pension policy which will mature at his normal retirement date. Therefore, instead of transferring the benefits to a new Occupational scheme, they go to a separate policy in the employee's name with the insurance company of his choice. This will give him some control over his pension and enable him to identify his scheme and follow its performance if he so wishes. It is, however, not possible for the member to pay any additional contributions to a Section 32 policy.

Part of the amounts paid to the Section 32 policy from a contracted-out scheme may go into a fixed-rate plan to provide the GMP. This fund is likely to grow at a slower rate than the rest of the fund which does not need to provide a guaranteed benefit and can be invested in a less constrained way. The main advantage of this form of policy is that the value of the fund (apart from the GMP element) should grow at a higher rate than that assumed by the actuary when calculating the transfer value. By using the Section 32 policy, the member will be giving up certain guaranteed benefits but is likely to gain from the higher, though not guaranteed, benefits. Also, the policy may be more flexible than the previous scheme on, for example, the earliest date that benefits may be received.

The Social Security Act 1985 goes further in this regard as it removes the need for the scheme rules to allow a Section 32 transfer payment. It obliges the trustees to make a transfer value of a member's benefits available to a Section 32 policy or to a new Occupational scheme if a member leaves service with a Deferred pension at least a year before his normal retirement date.

If the employee has made the decision to transfer his benefits into a Section 32 policy, his old employer will need to approach the scheme's actuary to ascertain the transfer value of those benefits. As you will be aware, there are many different ways to arrive at a solution and the answer will be arrived at after using various assumptions. Although the scheme's actuary will try to work out an equitable transfer value, he will want to protect the existing members of the scheme and the leaver may lose out if he has not taken professional advice. Advice is also required in selecting the insurance company which will manage the money to ensure that the investment performance will be sound.

Personal Pension Arrangements

One of the important selling points of the PPS is that it can be taken out independently of the employer and is fully portable so that it can be transferred to and from company schemes. The legislation states that, 'The Board shall not approve a PPS unless it makes provision for the making, accepting and application of transfer payments as satisfies any requirements imposed by or under regulations made by the Board.'

Section 17 of the Social Security Act 1986 allows existing provisions relating to Occupational pension schemes to be modified in consequence of the new PPS. The DHSS regulations:

— allow transfer values of rights from one PPS to another, or to an Occupational scheme;
— allow transfer values of rights in Occupational schemes to be paid to a PPS;
— allow a reduced transfer value to be provided by a contracted-out Money purchase scheme where the member's protected rights are not being transferred; and
— require an Occupational scheme to preserve the pension rights of a member who transfers the value of his PPS rights into the scheme. Any transfer value must be calculated in a manner approved by an actuary.

The DHSS regulations widen the scope for transfers of GMPS by allowing them to be the subject of transfer payments to an appropriate PPS and contracted-out Money purchase schemes (COMPS), provided the individual consents to the transfer which is used to provide Money purchase benefits. Protected rights in PPS and COMPS may be the subject of a transfer payment to another PPS or COMPS if the individual consents to the transfer, and if he is in employment covered by the scheme. The transfer payment will secure protected rights. Any COMPS will be required to provide the COMPS to which the individual was previously treated, as entitled in relation to the protected rights.

While the PPS allows for transfers to be made, the above problems of transferability could still be faced if he then moves in and out of an Occupational scheme. An individual could, in theory, negotiate for his new employer to contribute to his PPS which can continue to be funded personally. However, if the employer has a sound Group scheme he may be unwilling to contribute to a PPS as well, in which case the individual will have the choice between continuing to fund his PPS personally or transferring it into the Group scheme. If he transfers his PPS into a Group scheme the benefits of control and flexibility will be lost.

It is not possible to transfer a retirement annuity pension fund into an Occupational scheme and vice versa. This is because of the different rules which govern these schemes. If a self-employed person wishes to join an Occupational scheme, his only option is to make the retirement annuity policy paid up. Therefore, it will receive no more contributions but it can continue to grow tax-free and there should be no restriction on the rate of growth.

Chapter 12
Selecting Personal Pension Schemes

In the Chancellor of the Exchequer's Budget Speech on 17 March 1987, Nigel Lawson introduced the Personal pension schemes as:

> . . . an important dimension of ownership. They will enable employees – if they so wish – to opt out of their employer's schemes and make their own arrangements, tailored to fit their own circumstances, and they will provide a new opportunity for the 10 million employees who at present do not belong to an Occupational scheme to make provisions of their own and, if they so wish, to contract out of SERPS.

The introduction of the new Personal pension scheme ('PPS') followed the consultative document *Improving the pensions choice*, which was published in November 1986. It stated that the Government is committed to:

— giving people greater freedom of choice in how they provide for retirement; and
— removing pension barriers to job mobility.

The new legislation gives Personal pensions the same favourable tax treatment as is currently enjoyed by retirement annuities, and will be available to employees and the self-employed.

The starting date of the new PPS has been delayed from January 1988 to July 1988.

The principal aims of the new PPS are as follows:

1. To enable you to own your pension scheme.
You will have the right to full and regular information about the way your investment is performing.

2. To enable you to identify with your scheme.
It will be an individual arrangement so that it can be valued separately. Your pension fund is not part of an impersonal group arrangement and is not governed by the group scheme's rules.
3. To encourage job mobility.
As it is your pension scheme you should be able to take your pension with you when you change jobs without a penalty.
4. To enable you to choose how the fund is invested.
As it is your pension scheme you, rather than your employer, can choose the finance house which will manage your money unless it is already sponsored and set up by your employer.

The earliest retirement age has now been brought down to 50 making the pension scheme less of a long-term investment vehicle. However, the benefits at that age would be comparatively small.

The PPS will be funded on a money purchase basis, so if the benefits are taken early the pension will be much smaller. One of the problems with pensions is that they are often considered from the investment approach rather than the need to provide an adequate income stream in retirement. You will see from the calculations in Appendix 12 that the fund at 65 is worth approximately four times the value of the fund 10 years earlier. This is due to the additional contributions made and the investment returns over that period to bolster the fund.

Avoiding the Pitfalls

If you are not in a Company pension then you could use the PPS to form your own scheme. Whether this should be contracted-in to the State scheme or whether your PPS should take over responsibility for the SERPS pension will depend upon a number of factors particularly your age and the investment return expected from your PPS. These factors are dealt with in more detail in Chapter 7. If you contract out then you will be relieving the State of the burden of providing for your SERPS pension but this may not be wise if you are nearing retirement.

The new PPS has a number of welcome features, and will continue to receive much attention from the media as it has such a wide application. It will also be promoted by those who have a vested interest. The PPS features as part of the privatisation programme of the Conservative Government, and the Secretary of State for Social Services will be keen to promote the scheme to convey the Tory philosophy. The considerable direct sales forces of the life companies and the newcomers to the pensions world such as unit trusts, banks and building societies will be very keen to sign up clients under the new PPS due to the commissions involved, although under the Financial Services Act 1986 these are likely to be reduced. The benefits of the new PPS are likely to be well publicised but the pitfalls may not be so carefully examined.

In April 1987 the MORI poll reported that nearly two out of three employees consider that Personal pensions will offer a better deal than employers' schemes. Of the 1071 individuals interviewed in the sample, fewer than one in five thought that Company schemes were better. The poll showed that in 1987 more employees said that employers should make contributions towards the employees' Personal pensions.

The publicity relating to the PPS could have the following effects:

1. Employees could be persuaded to form their own PPS and leave their employer's scheme, even though the employer's scheme may be more likely to provide the greater benefits.
2. Employees may take on the State's liability to provide the

SERPS pension at a time when they are unlikely to be able to provide the same benefits.

3. Employees may become more critical of their employer's scheme and expect more from the pension scheme as a part of the salary package.

It is important that sound advice is taken before proceeding with any action; the following illustration shows that an employee may lose out by coming out of a good company scheme and setting up a PPS.

Table 12.1

A man aged 51 on a salary of £30,000 proposed to pay 14 per cent of his salary into a PPS. His salary escalates at 5 per cent per annum over this period to retirement and the fund grows at 10 per cent per annum:

	£
Personal pension scheme	
Value of fund	89,152
Pension using an annuity rate of (say) 12 per cent	10,698
Final salary scheme	
Maximum pension of two-thirds final salary £48,867 × 2/3	32,578

With the PPS publicity employers may need to take a defensive stance if they do wish to contribute to the employee's scheme. Certainly, it could be an administrative nightmare if the employer contributes and each employee were to use a different finance house to manage his PPS, with the employer contributing to numerous different schemes. If the employer is happy for his employee to take out a PPS it is more likely that a policy will be adopted whereby the employer will agree to the formation of a PPS with a small number of institutions. Indeed, some employers may insist that the scheme is set up through one finance house to keep the arrangement simple.

The employee can, of course, from 6 April 1988, insist that he leaves the employer's scheme to set up his own PPS on 1 July 1988. However, many employers take a paternalistic approach and wish to preserve the corporate image and strongly encourage the existing scheme. They should now be examining the scheme to ensure that it suffers from no deficiencies when compared with the PPS. If it is deficient then action may need to be taken. Often the employer's problem is that of communication and a public relations exercise may be required to explain the advantages of the existing scheme to the workforce. If an employee still wants to leave the Company scheme and set up his own PPS, the employer may feel less inclined to contribute to his new scheme at the same rate as before, or provide other fringe benefits which may be provided by the company such as permanent health insurance, medical insurance, life cover, etc.

For those who have never been in a pension scheme, the new arrangements allow them to contract out of SERPS, but they have always been able to provide for their own pensions through the Retirement annuity plan which is considered in more detail below.

The members of a Company scheme can now leave it to set up their own PPS. However, the employer is not obliged to contribute to the PPS, let alone at the same rate as before, provided a Company scheme already exists. Therefore, the employer's consent will often be required if the PPS is to be a practical alternative. Clearly, the message to any employee who is currently considering opting out of an Occupational arrangement into a PPS is 'look before you leap'.

Pension Contributions

The Inland Revenue will only approve a PPS if the contributions into the scheme are made by the following: the members; the employers; minimum contributions by the DHSS in respect of contracted-out schemes.

As the new PPS arrangement will be in force from 1 July 1988, the time-scale involved is very short. It is likely that the rules can be submitted and the scheme set up relatively quickly subject to Inland Revenue approval. The present indications are that the Inland Revenue would prefer to approve schemes on an interim basis and then deal with the detail at a later date, rather than delay the implementation of schemes beyond the start date of 1 July 1988.

The maximum level of contribution which may be made by the employee and be allowed for income tax purposes is as follows.

Table 12.2

Age at the beginning of the year of assessment	% of net relevant earnings
50 or younger	17.5
51-55	20.0
56-60	22.5
over 60	27.5

Table 12.3

A woman aged 40 has net relevant earnings of £40,000 per annum. Her company contributes £3,000 per annum to her PPS.

	£
Maximum contribution £40,000 × 17.5 per cent	7,000
Less contribution by employer	(3,000)
Maximum allowable payment by employee for income tax purposes	4,000

Selecting Personal Pension Schemes

If the employer contributes to the PPS then the limits in Table 12.2 shall be reduced by those contributions. The definition of net relevant earnings is set out in Appendix 13.

The following illustration shows the tax relief which may be receivable if both the employer and employee contribute to the PPS.

Table 12.4

Facts as per the previous example assuming that tax is paid at the top rate by both employer and employee.

	Company £	*Employee* £	*Total* £
Gross contribution	3,000	4,000	7,000
Tax relief 35/60 per cent	(1,050)	(2,400)	(3,450)
Net contribution	1,950	1,600	3,550

If beneficial, an individual can elect within three months of the end of a year of assessment, in which a payment is made under a PPS, for that payment to be treated as paid:

(a) in the previous year of assessment; or
(b) if he had no net relevant earnings in that previous year of assessment, in the year of assessment before that; or
(c) in the next year of assessment, but two if an individual has net relevant earnings as an underwriting member of Lloyd's or by way of commissions calculated by reference to the profits of Lloyd's underwriting business, and there is unused relief in respect of the earnings.

If the Government continues with its policy of reducing personal taxes then this election may be more widely used.

For those who have not made full use of their maximum relief in respect of a Personal pension contribution in any year, it is possible to carry forward the unused relief and

Table 12.5

A man aged 40 pays £3,000 to his PPS. His marginal rate of tax on that payment in the current year is 50 per cent but due to exceptional income in the previous year his top rate of tax was 60 per cent. The tax rates used are those for 1987/88 in both cases.

	£	£
Year of payment		
Pension payment	3,000	–
Tax relief at 50 per cent	(1,500)	(1,500)
Net payment	1,500	–
Election for carry back		
Pension payment	3,000	–
Tax relief at 60 per cent	(1,800)	1,800
Net payment	1,200	–
Benefit from election		300

obtain tax relief in respect of any pension contributions paid in any of the next six years of assessment as exceeds the maximum applying for that year. Relief is given on a 'first in, first out' basis (ie relief for earlier years being exhausted before that for a later year). Where there is unused relief and an assessment becomes final and conclusive more than six years after the end of that year, you have six months from the date of the assessment to pay further contributions and elect for them to be carried back to the year with unused relief. In practice, a premium paid within six months of a letter of offer under an Inland Revenue investigation will normally be allowed for tax purposes.

The PPS arrangement will be operated in a similar way to the MIRAS scheme under which mortgage payments are made. The Personal pension contributions will be made net of basic-rate tax. The scheme administrator will then recover

Table 12.6

A man received remuneration as set out below. He pays 12 per cent per annum into his PPS and he makes a further payment of £5,000 in year seven to take account of part of the unused relief.

Year	Remun-eration £	Maximum relief £	Personal payments £	Unused relief £	'Top-up' £	Revised unused relief £
1	22,000	3,850	2,640	1,210	1,210	–
2	23,000	4,025	2,760	1,265	1,265	–
3	24,250	4,244	2,910	1,334	875	459
4	25,500	4,462	3,060	1,402	–	1,402
5	27,000	4,725	3,240	1,485	–	1,485
6	28,500	4,988	3,420	1,568	–	1,568
7	30,000	5,250	3,600	1,650	1,650	–
	180,250	31,544	21,630	9,914	5,000	4,914

the basic rate of tax from the Inland Revenue and pay it into the scheme. In this way basic-rate taxpayers will receive their relief at source. Higher-rate taxpayers will need to

Table 12.7

A 60 per cent taxpayer makes a gross monthly payment of £200 under the PPS.

	£
Monthly contribution paid by employee £200 at 73 per cent	146
Basic rate of tax recovered by scheme administrator £200 at 27 per cent	54
Amount actually invested	200
Higher-rate relief coded in £200 at 33 per cent	66

have the higher-rate relief coded in so that it can be taken into account when they receive their salary.

Minimum Contributions and Protected Rights

The minimum contributions paid into the PPS by the DHSS will represent the aggregate of:

(a) the difference between the full rate of national insurance contributions and the reduced contracted-out rate; and
(b) a tax credit at the basic rate of income tax on the employee's share of the NIC rebate; and
(c) the 2 per cent 'special incentive' payment.

These contributions will buy protected rights based on the following:

(a) a pension only (no tax-free cash) will be payable based on unisex and unistatus annuity rates payable from age 65 for men and age 60 for women;
(b) there must be provision for a 50 per cent spouse's pension on death after retirement;
(c) a spouse's pension based on the value of the fund in the event of death before retirement;
(d) the pension must be subject to an increase of 3 per cent per annum or the RPI if less.

Benefits

The PPS fund will roll-up tax-free to produce the following benefits:

1. A pension to the member.

2. A tax-free lump sum.
3. A pension to the widow, widower or dependant or a lump sum to the estate.
4. A death-in-service lump sum.

The pension may be taken at any time from age 50 (or earlier under the special circumstances of incapacity). It has been said that the new legislation brings forward the normal retirement date from 65 to 50 for men and from 60 to 50 for women. This is not necessarily true as it has always been possible, with consent, to retire early at 50 and take lower benefits. Since the new PPS will be funded on a money purchase basis you will only get out of the scheme what you put in, subject to the investment returns, so that again lower benefits will be received if the scheme runs to age 50 rather than 60, as it will have been funded for fewer years and the annuity rate will be based upon a younger person. The pension will normally be for life although it could be for a period of less than 10 years (notwithstanding the member's death within that term) if preferred, although a pension for life would be the most usual term. The pension cannot be assigned or surrendered unless in the unusual circumstances that it is a pension for a set period which may be assigned upon death.

The tax-free cash sum, which cannot be assigned or surrendered, must not exceed:

(a) 25 per cent of the value of the fund when it is paid; or
(b) £150,000 or such other figure as is specified by an order made by the Treasury from time to time.

At present the legislation relates the £150,000 limit to a policy rather than an individual. Therefore if you have a number of separate plans, it is possible to obtain more than £150,000 of cash. This is surely not what was intended and could be changed by future legislation. However, introducing such legislation may be difficult because if the limit were to be related to the individual it would be difficult for the Inland Revenue to police the rules. As the PPS produces tax-free cash (unlike new AVC arrangements) it is likely to be widely used for pension mortgages.

In general it would be advisable for an individual to have more than one personal pension plan so as to spread the risks of poor management and provide for a greater choice of investment. Also by operating a small number of personal pension schemes rather than just one, more than £150,000 of tax-free cash can be extracted as illustrated below.

Table 12.8

A man aged 45 has net relevant earnings of £60,000. His earnings increase at 5 per cent per annum and he pays 16 per cent of his earnings each year into two personal pension schemes which both grow at the rate of 10 per cent per annum. He takes his benefits at 65.

	Scheme 1 £	Scheme 2 £	Total £
If two schemes are operated			
Accumulated fund	430,236	430,236	860,472
Maximum tax-free cash — 25 per cent of fund	107,559	107,559	215,118
If one scheme is operated			
Accumulated fund	860,472		860,472
Maximum tax-free cash — 25 per cent of fund restricted to	150,000		150,000
Additional tax-free cash from operating two policies (£215,118 — 150,000)			65,118

Selecting Personal Pension Schemes

The terms of the dependant's pension are set out in Appendix 14. A lump sum payment may be made on the death if the member dies before attaining age 75. Therefore if he defers taking the pension, he can roll-up the fund as this can enable a lump sum to be paid free of inheritance tax to his dependants. The maximum premiums that may be paid by the member in any year of assessment to secure this benefit is 5 per cent of his net relevant earnings. As previously mentioned, premiums which produce life cover provide the most tax-efficient form of life assurance.

The maximum permitted Death-in-service payment under an Occupational pension scheme is four times final salary. As the PPS is funded on a money purchase basis, if the maximum payment of 5 per cent of net relevant earnings is made each year, the benefits could exceed four times salary. However, normally a member will be funding for a pension for him and his wife rather than the lump sum payment on death.

Job Mobility

With a Personal pension scheme there is no bar to job mobility, provided your new employer is happy to continue your PPS at the same rate as your previous employer. If not, you may need to reconsider your PPS and possibly join and start contributing to your new employer's scheme. The benefits will accordingly be received from your PPS and your employer's new scheme.

The new Personal pension scheme is likely to be more attractive for the younger employees who are in mobile employment (eg advertising, oil and computer software industries) and for those who are unlikely to join an employer's scheme.

The Pension Providers

Traditionally only life offices could offer to run a Personal scheme or a scheme for smaller companies. Since the Government is anxious to produce greater competition in the financial services industry it has now widened the definition of pension providers to include life offices, banks, building societies, unit trusts and friendly societies.

Although the above institutions may run pension schemes, the annuities will continue to be provided exclusively by life offices because only life offices can accept mortality risks and guarantees. Therefore a unit trust could operate a pension scheme but the individual must return to a life office to provide the pension.

It is expected that many of the leaders in the above sectors will be lured to offer Personal pension schemes as they are expected to be a lucrative source of business. However, these institutions will be under pressure to set up systems to cope with the influx of work once the PPS becomes available from 1 July 1988. The cost of setting up these systems is likely to be very substantial.

The Financial Services legislation has posed a problem for banks and building societies. In the past the bank manager has been viewed as an independent intermediary by the public and has been able to encourage clients to take the bank's products. However, if the banks continue to promote their own products they will no longer be able to act as independent intermediaries, unless they can prove that their products are better in performance terms.

Chapter 13
The Self-employed Approach

In the past the self-employed and employees who are not members of a pension scheme have been able to pay into a retirement annuity contract ('RAP contract'), the legislation for which is governed by sections 226 to 229 ICTA 1970. The self-employed are allowed to pay premiums based on net relevant earnings from any trade, profession, vocation, office or employment. This also includes patent rights which are treated as earned income. All sole traders and partners of trading and professional practices (eg surveyors and solicitors) come within this category. Retirement annuity contracts will cease to be available from 1 July 1988 (they will be replaced by the new Personal pension scheme) although individuals who already have RAP contracts at that time will be able to continue contributing to them.

Personal Pension Schemes

The self-employed can join the new PPS, from 1 July 1988 when the PPS arrangements will replace the RAP contracts. When considering annual premiums which attract the maximum tax relief, retirement annuity premiums and those paid into a PPS will need to be aggregated. While the basic structure of the RAP contract for the self-employed is similar to the PPS (as set out above) there are the following main differences:

1. A RAP contract may only be with a life office or friendly society whereas a PPS may be with other finance houses such as banks, building societies, unit trusts, etc., therefore the investment areas of the PPS are wider.

2. A pension can normally only be taken from age 60 under a retirement annuity while the PPS enables the pension to be taken from age 50.

3. The tax-free lump sum cannot exceed three times the pension payable under the RAP contract rather than 25 per cent of the value of the accumulated fund under a PPS. The existing RAP contracts which were effected before 17 March 1987 do not restrict tax-free cash to £150,000 unlike the new PPS. (However, any RAP contract which is established between 17 March 1987 and 1 July 1988 will not produce tax-free cash in excess of £150,000.)

Table 13.1

A man retires at 60 with a pension fund of £680,000 and wishes to take the maximum tax-free cash and pension. Annuity rates are, say, 12 per cent.

	Retirement annuity £	*Personal pension scheme* £
Pension if no tax-free cash taken	81,600	81,600
Fund	680,000	680,000
Maximum tax-free cash £60,000 (see below) × 3	(180,000)	–
25 per cent of £680,000 restricted to £150,000	–	(150,000)
Fund used to buy pension	500,000	530,000
Pension per annum, if maximum tax-free cash taken £500,000/ £530,000 × 12 per cent	60,000	63,600
Plus tax-free cash of	180,000	150,000

4. Premiums are payable gross under a retirement annuity contract, the tax relief being claimed by the individual on his tax return, whereas an employee may pay net into a PPS contract and claim higher-rate relief through a coding notice following submission of his tax return.

In most other respects the RAP contract is similar to the PPS arrangement, the details of which have been described above. These include the level of pension contributions, the election to carry back premiums for tax purposes, the carry forward of unused relief for six years and the benefits to be derived. The access to tax-free cash can enable an interest-only loan of up to 15 times the annual premium to be obtained which may be used in arranging a pension-linked mortgage.

In the Parliamentary debates, the Financial Secretary, Mr. Norman Lamont said, 'Existing retirement annuities will continue on the same basis, but I am advised that they will be able to convert to Personal pension plans. That is all that I can tell my Hon. Friend at this stage . . .' This would appear to enable, for example, an individual to take benefits from an existing Retirement annuity plan earlier than is normally possible.

Maximum Funding

The higher earning self-employed have, in the past, been at a disadvantage as regards funding for maximum benefits. Although they may now pay 17.5 per cent of Net Relevant Earnings ('NRE'), or more if over 50, into a RAP or PPS contract, in the past the maximum limits were restricted by a ceiling which may have prevented them from contributing at their required level. The rates (ignoring those for older contributors) were as follows:

1971/72 to 1975/76	15% of NRE up to £1,500
1976/77	15% of NRE up to £2,250
1977/78 to 1979/80	15% of NRE up to £3,000
1980/81 onwards	17.5% of NRE

These restrictions may make it more important for such individuals to ensure that they are adequately provided for in retirement.

Table 13.2

A man aged 60 on 1 January 1987 has been making provision for retirement since he was 45. His share of profits in 1971/72 was £100,000 and these have increased at 10 per cent per annum.

	£
Maximum premiums paid 1971/72 to 1986/87	111,306
Maximum premiums using current rates	155,134

Tax-free Cash

As mentioned above, the method of computing tax-free cash may be more advantageous under the existing RAP rules than under the PPS arrangement so that urgent action may be required before 1 July 1988. Under the RAP arrangement, in order to maximise the tax-free cash (free, that is, from income tax or capital gains tax), the cheapest possible annuity rate may be used. The tax-free cash of three times this annuity is then taken. The residual fund may then be used to provide a pension on a very different basis. The PPS arrangement avoids this form of abuse by allowing tax-free cash of no more than 25 per cent of the fund (see Table 13.3).

The Self-employed Approach

From Financial Times Business Information comes the largest selling pensions magazine in the UK.

Pensions Management.

Every month:

- ★ With updated performance statistics on most individual pension funds in the UK
- ★ With an in depth survey on a key aspect of the pensions industry every month (Self Employed Pensions, Executive Pensions, AVCs and many more)
- ★ With articles on aspects of the pensions market place often neglected in the more general financial press.
- ★ With news
- ★ With reviews

Written by professionals for professionals.

If you're reading this book, you should be reading Pensions Management every month.

For a free back issue and subscription details, write to:
Marketing Department, Pensions Management, FTBI, Greystoke Place, Fetter Lane, London EC4A 1ND.

Table 13.3

	£	£
A man retires at 60 with a pension fund of	200,000	–
RAP arrangement		
Level pension payable annually in arrear without any guarantee, Widow's pension or protection on early death (say, 13 per cent)	26,000	–
Tax-free cash taken £26,000 × 3		78,000
Residual fund £200,000−78,000 =£122,000 used to buy pension increasing at 8.5 per cent with Widow's pension and five-year guarantee (say, 9 per cent)	10,980	–
Tax-free cash over seven times pension		
PPS		
Tax-free cash 25 per cent of fund £200,000	–	50,000
Pension say £150,000 at (say, 9 per cent)	13,500	

Inheritance Tax

The opportunity to write death benefits by way of a flexible trust is important as it could save inheritance tax. This is because the benefit can pass outside the estate to members of the family. If the benefits pass to the spouse (and this may be necessary for financial reasons) then inheritance tax will still be payable on the death of the survivor, but if they pass into trust for the children then the funds would not attract inheritance tax until the death of the children.

Life Assurance

Life assurance is extremely important for the self-employed. The ability to pay up to 5 per cent of premiums into a term assurance policy so as to protect the family should death occur before retirement is crucial.

As income tax relief may be received, it makes this form of life assurance one of the cheapest available.

Table 13.4

Annual cost of life cover of £100,000 up to age 60 for a man who is now aged 45 is, say, £500.

	Self-employed paying tax at		
	27%	*45%*	*60%*
	£	£	£
Gross premium	500	500	500
Tax relief	(135)	(225)	(300)
Net cost	365	275	200

Doctors and Dentists

Doctors and dentists are in a unique position. They are normally taxed under income tax Schedule D and are therefore able to pay part of their earnings into a PPS. However, they are also required to be members of and contribute to the National Health Service Superannuation Scheme ('NHSSS') in relation to any NHS work and are also

The Daily Telegraph Pensions Guide

Table 13.5

A doctor contributes £600 to the NHSSS
Estimate of pensionable earnings £600 × 100/6 = £10,000

in pensionable employment. As they are normally taxed on the preceding year's basis, to avoid considerable delay in arriving at the pensionable earnings, an estimate is made and this is normally based on the amount paid to the NHSSS. As the contribution is normally 6 per cent the pensionable earnings are normally grossed up accordingly.

Table 13.6

A GP aged 35 is a top-rate taxpayer. She has net relevant earnings of £50,000 and pays £600 into the NHSSS.

	£	£
Option 1		
Earnings	50,000	–
Less pensionable earnings £600 × 100/6	(10,000)	–
	40,000	–
PPS premium £40,000 × 17.5 per cent	7,000	–
Tax relief at 60 per cent		4,200
Add tax relief on NHSSS payment £600 at 60 per cent		360
		4,560
Option 2		
Earnings	50,000	–
PPS premium at 17.5 per cent	8,750	–
Tax relief at 60 per cent		5,250

A GP has two options:

1. By concession, he can claim tax relief on the NHSSS contributions and disregard the pensionable earnings for PPS and RAP purposes, or
2. The GP can pay PPS premiums based on latest (including pensionable) earnings but not claim concessional relief on NHSSS contributions paid.

The latter option may be advantageous as the NHSSS pay will provide a pension and it can be used again to maximise pension payments.

A practitioner who is considering increasing his pension benefits could pay additional voluntary contributions to purchase added years under the NHSSS, which may be attractive as the NHSSS currently inflation proofs pensions (although the retirement annuity route affords greater flexibility and life assurance benefits).

Overseas Income

Overseas income normally falls into three categories:

1. Not chargeable to UK tax. This will normally be the case if the individual is not resident in the UK, in which case retirement annuity premiums cannot attract tax relief.
2. Chargeable to UK tax but subject to the 100 per cent deduction. Schedule E taxpayers may be eligible for the 100 per cent deduction if approximately 10 months out of 12 are spent abroad. This period does not necessarily need to fall within a fiscal year. The income can be used to fund a retirement annuity premium, but other UK income may need to be received to enable UK tax relief to be claimed.
3. Chargeable to UK tax with no deduction in which case any retirement annuity premium would attract tax relief.

Waiver of Premiums

It is becoming popular for RAP policies to include a waiver of premium benefit. In the event of incapacity, contributions could be waived and the retirement benefits will be protected as if the contributions had continued to be paid. It may be that a separate permanent health policy will produce income during the period of incapacity. Also, the retirement annuity contract could include provisions for a lifetime disability.

The waiver of premium cost will normally be 2 to 5 per cent of the premium, and it will be fully eligible for income tax relief.

Self-managed Schemes

In recent years certain insurance companies have issued self-managed policies so that the self-employed can obtain the same benefits of self-management as controlling directors through their Self-administered schemes. The self-employed can determine the investment strategy, including the purchase of business premises of the partnership. While this arrangement is often attractive it can cause problems for retiring partners whose retirement annuity contract could largely consist of the premises he is leaving.

Chapter 14
Focus on Investment

As we have seen, the combination of tax relief and good management should make the pension fund the best performing investment vehicle. The investment performance is a key factor because of the long-term nature of a pension fund, which is too often overlooked or monitored in a haphazard way. If you have a share portfolio you may study the *Financial Times* on a daily basis to follow the price of your shares but ignore an asset which may ultimately be more valuable to you, your pension fund. Regular monitoring of the fund is required so that you can take action where necessary. If one fund manager is consistently underperforming it may be advisable to switch investment house and ensure that all future and past contributions are managed differently. Therefore professional advice should be sought.

Since the late 1970s we have seen one of the longest consistent bull markets in the history of the UK Stock Exchange. This has meant that while certain companies were making contributions into their pension schemes at a certain level to produce maximum benefits for members, based on annual growth of say 15 per cent per annum, the fund may have performed at twice that level. This has led to a number of schemes being over-funded. As such schemes are so tax-efficient the Chancellor of the Exchequer introduced legislation in 1986 to avoid this abuse, as explained earlier in this book.

The investment performance can greatly distort funding levels.

Table 14.1

A man retires at 60 on a final salary of £20,000 per annum. His salary has increased at 5 per cent per annum and annual pension contributions have been made since 40 at 10 per cent of salary.

	£
Final salary	20,000
Pension (ignoring tax-free cash) at 2/3	13,333
Fund required to produce £13,333 per annum (say)	111,000

	Fund grown at the rate of	
	10% per annum	15% per annum
	£	£
Fund required	111,000	111,000
Value of fund	71,000	139,000
Over/(under) funding	(40,000)	28,000

You can see that a growth rate of 10 per cent per annum in this example has not enabled the scheme to fund for maximum benefits, while a growth rate of 15 per cent per annum has produced overfunding.

Managed Schemes

The vast majority of Personal and smaller Company pension schemes are managed by insurance companies. The choice of company is vast and too often it is the company with the best advertising rather than best performance which attracts the most money.

Focus on Investment

Table 14.2

£1,000 single premium invested in the pension fund managed sector.

	Value of fund after 5 years £	Average annual compound growth rate %	Value of fund £m
Irish Life Managed	3,997	32	4.0
Target Life	3,875	31	192.3
NPI Managed	3,544	29	54.7
FT Ind Ord Index	3,129	26	–
Albany	3,023	25	92.0
Average for managed sector	2,788	23	–
Allied Dunbar	2,622	21	1,448.0
Abbey Life	2,311	18	427.6

Source: Money Management, June 1987

This chart shows the performance over a five-year period of a few of the life assurance companies which were quoted in the June 1987 issue of *Money Management*. It shows that investment selection is crucial as there can be a wide differential between the performance of various companies.

Too often an investment house is selected with those responsible for the pension scheme failing to monitor the performance and compare it with competitors. However, it is also important not to overreact as an investment house should be given sufficient time to prove itself.

When considering the general investment performance of a life company, it is important to examine its track record throughout the various sectors and over a long period through bull and bear markets. For example, Allied Dunbar managed fund is seen as slightly below the sector average of five years, but over the last three years their Far Eastern fund is one of the leaders of the sector which was headed by Albany Life. Target Life is one of the sector leaders largely due to a decision in the 1980s to go heavily into UK equities rather than maintain a more balanced portfolio. The performance of the sector (average annual compound growth rate 23 per cent) should be viewed against the bull market of the 1980s. The FT Industrial Ordinary Index represents UK stocks whereas the managed sector invests only part of the funds into the UK equity market.

When examining the past, pensions statistics need careful examination. It is normally prudent to examine the long-term record of a company which has performed during good and bad markets. For example, Table 14.3 shows that the new funds in the short term have performed better than the older funds over the longer term.

You will see that the newer funds are able to boast much higher returns but, of course, these have been made during favourable market conditions whereas the older funds have had to battle through the bear markets. It is also easier for a young fund with a relatively small fund size to offer special prices and take more risks to try to climb to the top of league tables, when launching its fund. When looking at the past performance, many brokers will favour the investment house which is consistently able to perform well, being found in the upper reaches of league tables though not necessarily coming first.

While the past performance of an investment company is a guide, it is not the key to the future. Too much emphasis is placed upon past rather than future performance. If a company has performed badly, there may be a good reason. It may, for example, have just recruited a team of leading financial analysts who could take the company from the lower leagues into the first division. If choosing an investment house was as easy as reviewing the financial

Table 14.3

Recent managed funds (top performing)	Annual return from launch %	Launch date	Fund size £m
Royal London Mixed	61.3	Oct 86	0.5
TSB Managed	50.3	Nov 84	19.2
Devonshire Life	49.9	Feb 86	0.8
CML Rainbow Managed	46.6	Jan 84	2.4
Commercial Union	43.8	Jan 84	15.2
Pre-March 1974 managed funds			
N M Schroder	21.0	Jan 74	111.1
Save & Prosper	20.4	Feb 74	94.1
Allied Dunbar	17.6	Apr 71	1,448.0
Confederation Life	16.8	Jan 73	124.2
Imperial Life Canada	12.9	Feb 72	83.6

Source: *Pensions Management*, June 1987

magazines such as *Money Management* and *Pensions Management*, then some brokers would be out of a job. It is obviously not that simple and the best guide to the future is not only information on past performance but also detailed knowledge of the current investment teams, their investment strategy and any future changes which may take place.

The Sector

Apart from the selection of the investment house, the sector selection is also vital. This will often be left to the investment manager but you should have some input on the decision as it should reflect your own investment philosophy. In general terms, the greater the opportunities for capital appreciation, the higher the risk. Therefore if you are looking for high capital growth and accept the risk element you may be happy for the funds to remain in the more volatile sectors, such as the Far Eastern fund. If you are very cautious you may want the money to be invested in, say, the money market or gilts funds. Often, a mix of the two extremes is preferred. The managed fund, for example, is a mix of investments into the other sectors at the fund manager's discretion.

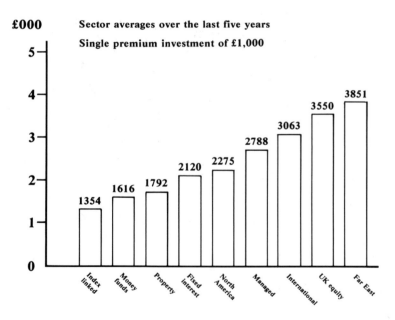

Figure 14.1 *Source: Money Management, June 1987*

The performance of the various sectors should be viewed against the long-term bull market of the early 1980s. For example, the managed fund sector grew by an average of 23 per cent per annum and the UK equity sector by almost

Focus on Investment

29 per cent per annum. This growth is unlikely to continue over a longer term. The performance will vary enormously but, for illustrative purposes only, the investment could be spread among the various sectors as follows.

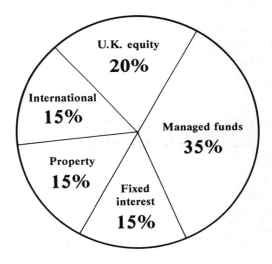

Figure 14.2

Unit-linked contracts

A unit-linked fund means that its value is related to the value of the stocks and shares which have been acquired, therefore the fund rises and falls in line with the underlying shares. The manager's job is to recognise when to buy and sell a particular share and when to come in and out of a sector. Table 14.4 illustrates the choice of sectors within the unit-linked market.

Table 14.4

Unit-linked funds at June 1987.

	No of funds
Managed	111
UK equity	107
International	79
Property	68
Money market	97
Fixed interest	73
European	27
Index-linked	39
Far East	45
North America	40
Total	686

Source: Money Management, June 1987

With-profit contracts

In addition to the above unit-linked funds, there are 30 to 40 companies operating traditional with-profit funds. People often become more prudent as retirement draws near. You may be happy for the funds to be in the riskier sectors earlier in your career, but not wish to jeopardise the accumulated fund when you are only, say, five years from taking your benefits. This may be the time to switch from the unit-linked into the with-profit market.

The with-profit policy may guarantee that the fund upon maturity will not be less than the money paid into it plus a small rate of return. The return is based on a number of factors including performance and the company's reserves and tends to be given in three parts:

(a) the guaranteed return — this is normally declared from the outset;
(b) the annual bonus — is not normally guaranteed in advance and tends to be relatively low;
(c) the terminal bonus — is given at the end of the contract. It can fluctuate widely from company to company and is given having regard to the performance of the fund.

Once the annual bonus has been given, it cannot be taken away. If the performance has been very poor then no bonus may be received. Normally with-profit contracts will not perform as well as a unit-linked policy but they may give you the additional security you are seeking.

Comparative Investments

As mentioned earlier in this book the tax advantages of a pension fund should ensure that it will outperform most comparative personal investments. However, if the pension fund monies are well managed, the picture can become even more remarkable.

Table 14.5 compares the performance of a building society deposit account against a good pension fund performance. The building society deposit account comprises an investment of £10,000 made 15 years ago. It is assumed that interest has been credited to the account each year and the higher-rate tax charge has been paid out of the account. It is further assumed that the taxpayer was paying tax at the top rate of 60 per cent throughout the period. In comparison, a pension fund contribution of £25,000 was made into the M & G personal UK equity fund (a good performer in the sector over 15 years) which, after tax relief, cost £10,000.

Table 14.5

	Initial investment £	Value after 15 years £	Average/ annual growth after 15 years %
Building society deposit	10,000	19,140	4.5
M & G pension fund			
— net investment	10,000	–	–
— tax relief	15,000	–	–
— gross investment	25,000	328,900	19.0

You will see from the above that the figures are staggering. I have selected a period of 15 years for this comparison as this takes into account the bear market of the 1970s. Clearly we have seen one of the most prolonged bull markets during the early to mid-1980s and an average return of 19 per cent cannot be expected in a falling market.

Commission

The charging structure for brokers falls into a number of different categories. Some brokers are tied agents and act exclusively for one company. They receive a salary together with commission based upon the sales they are able to achieve. Other brokers are known as independent intermediaries and are not tied to any one company, and their income is based upon commission from various finance houses. These brokers do not charge their clients a fee. Others, such as accountants, charge a fee and will also retain part of the appropriate commission in some instances.

In April 1987, the DHSS announced that it was intended that administrative charges for the new PPS will not be controlled in the expectation that charges will stabilise at acceptable levels as a result of competition and disclosure. That remains to be seen!

It appears that one effect of the Financial Services Act 1986 has been to reduce commission rates. This level of commission will depend upon whether the client is committed to continuous payment or whether it is a one-off single premium payment.

The following illustration indicates the approximate level of commission which may be payable.

Table 14.6

Broker's commission from a pension contribution of £10,000 for an individual aged 40 who will be retiring at 60.

		Regular premium £	Single premium £
Year 1	Initial commission		
	2.5 per cent × £10,000 × 20 years	5,000	–
	4 per cent × £10,000	–	400
Year 2-20	2.5 per cent × £10,000 × 18	4,500	–
	4 per cent × £10,000 × 19	–	7,600
		9,500	8,000

In the above example, under the regular premium contract, the commission of £5,000 would be spread over two years and the continuous commission of £250 per annum would be paid from year three (ie £4,500). The above example does not reflect the true picture as it does not illustrate the effect on cash flow which again favours the broker who arranges a regular premium contract.

You will also see from the above example that for a man with 20 years until retirement, about half the first year's premium could go in commission. This would affect the performance of the fund in the short term. For a man with 40 years to retirement the first year's premium could go entirely in commission, although this is now unlikely!

Group company schemes are likely to suffer lower charges due to the sums involved. Since the front-loaded charges can range from 5 to 8 per cent it is advisable to seek advice and ensure that the charges are reasonable, enabling substantial savings to be made. For the large schemes substantial savings can be made from a Group scheme rather than having individuals setting up their own regular premium arrangements.

As mentioned above, the commissions and charges are likely to change following the impact of the Financial Services Act 1986. It is difficult at this time to determine what the long-term position will be, but we should get a better picture in the very near future.

The charges of a Self-administered pension scheme can be smaller than that of an Insured scheme depending upon the level of contribution. It is not normally worth setting up a scheme if the contribution will be less than about £15,000. However, once the annual payments are in the region of £20,000 and above, the costs should be reduced.

The New Players

In the past the investment of pension funds has been the domain of the insurance companies, but now banks, building societies and friendly societies will be allowed to enter the Personal pension scheme arena. This will provide a wider choice and will make the pensions market even more competitive.

The purchase of an annuity at retirement is a different proposition from the investment of the funds pre-retirement. The pension payable is based on actuarial statistics of life expectancy and interest rates at the date the annuity is purchased. It will vary depending upon the type of pension taken (eg does it include a Widow's pension?). Life offices will continue to be the only institution which can provide this service, so while you may invest your pension funds with a bank you will need to take your pension from a life office.

The Open-market Option

At normal retirement age, most pension schemes must give you an open-market option. This applies to both Occupational and Personal schemes. It means that even though the pension scheme may have been run by an insurance company, your pension does not have to come from that company. This is an important option which is often overlooked. The insurance company may have managed the scheme well but it may not be offering the best annuity rates, so by shopping around you could receive a higher pension. This is a highly competitive market and professional advice at this stage will almost certainly result in a higher pension in retirement.

The open-market option must also be provided in respect of the protected rights from contracting out of SERPS, but the company that provides the protected rights annuity must be one which offers it on a 'unisex basis'.

Chapter 15
Seeking Impartial Advice

As mentioned earlier, this book has been written as a practical guide rather than a technical textbook. It is intended to explain the benefits of pension schemes and the available options, but identifying an area where action should be taken is just the first step. You may then need professional advice before proceeding further.

The need for and benefit of pension schemes has led to the creation of an industry which depends upon the investment of funds for its survival. The lucrative commissions which are paid to professional intermediaries (such as independent advisors, accountants and tied-insurance agents) to encourage them to invest their client's money with that investment house clearly makes it more difficult to find impartial advice. Sorting through your post will reveal that there is no shortage of those who are willing to offer advice, but to whom should you turn?

The Financial Services Act 1986

Apart from the charging commission structure, one of the implications of the Financial Services Act 1986 is that it is much more difficult for an advisor to claim impartiality if he is linked to a finance house as a tied agent. It is now necessary to declare any such linkage so that it should now be possible to distinguish between the respective advisors and select those who are genuinely independent. In April 1987 the MORI poll showed that the most common source to whom people would turn for pensions advice is the bank manager, while the majority of employees did not know where they could go for advice.

However, the bank manager who has not been trained to understand the intricacies of the different pension arrangements will turn to advice from Head Office, which will inevitably be strongly geared towards that bank's own Personal pension scheme. This is not to infer that a bank manager will not provide his client with the best advice, but that there will undoubtedly be a conflict of interest.

The smaller broker who relies heavily on the sale of different insurance companies' products for his income will, sadly for the public who relies on a personal efficient service in most cases, find it more difficult in the current climate. The new regulations, administration, expenses and Government red tape will make it difficult for him to operate. He may be inclined to give up his independence and join a financial services organisation as a tied agent, as the costs of complying with the new Government regulations may be too onerous. This potential loss of independent advice will doubtless affect the current wide choice for employees, employers and the self-employed.

The Financial Services Act 1986 should streamline the number of organisations which are able to remain impartial. Although the numbers will be reduced, it is as important as ever to make the right choice.

Points to Consider

The areas for which advice should be sought have been covered in this book. The following is a summary of some of the more important matters which are likely to need further consideration:

1. The structuring or restructuring of a pension scheme; the available choices.
2. The level of pension contributions
3. Contracting out of the State scheme.
4. The range of benefits which should be provided.
5. The investment performance and choice of company.
6. The cost structure.
7. The pension options on changing jobs.
8. Investment of lump sum and receipt of pension upon retirement.
9. The open-market option.

Impartial Advisors

It is essential that you receive sound impartial advice from those who are sufficiently experienced because of the complexity of pensions legislation, the numerous choices which are available and the need to ensure that your money is invested well. But to whom can you turn? Obviously, there are always exceptions to every rule and so the following should be regarded as a general guideline.

As mentioned above, people often turn to their bank manager but he will not always be sufficiently knowledgeable of the complex pension rules or even impartial. The life offices (and in the future the banks and other financial institutions) are able to field very experienced pensions specialists. Some are able to provide a good comprehensive service, with their advice extending to tax. Also, would a direct salesman who is linked to one company be interested in selling the financial products of another company, even when they are clearly better?

The specialist pension brokers and consultants are more likely to provide you with the best advice. They fall into two categories, those who are tied to one finance house and those who are independent intermediaries. The former suffer from the same problem as the direct salesman – they can only recommend one company's products. The latter, however, can give you their advice on all the products in the market.

One of the sad implications of the Financial Services Act 1986 is that it is likely to squeeze out some of the reputable small brokers who are able to give both impartial and personal advice. It will leave the field more open to the large companies with their own hired workforce. Even so, good brokers both large and small can still be found. You should enquire into the reputation and experience of the broker and also ask for details of their charging structure, because some brokers will charge on a fee basis for special work while others rely solely on commission received for the sale. You should ask how much commission is to be received and, if you are unhappy, seek a second opinion before proceeding with a contract.

The consulting actuary will often work on a fee basis but is more likely to be called in by employers who need advice on the structure of the pension scheme rather than the employee. The actuary may also be more experienced in Self-administered schemes than the whole range of pension arrangements. However, unless the actuary knows the pensions market well, and has set up a personal financial planning section, he may only be able to advise on the structure of a scheme rather than the best financial house.

The solicitor may be able to assist in the legal work which is connected with the implementation of a pension scheme. One point to remember is that, unlike accountants, solicitors are prohibited from retaining any commissions generated but have to discount such commission (unless under £10) from the fee they charge. They are closely supervised by the Law Society and also have to carry indemnity insurance.

This brings us to the chartered accountant. Over the last few years there has been a trend towards certain firms of

Seeking Impartial Advice

accountants creating a personal financial planning section which will include specialists from the pensions and life assurance industry. Those with a specialist team should be able to provide sound advice on various alternatives and general structure of a scheme. Again you should enquire into whether they are likely to be commission-led and seek references. Accountants are required to inform their client of any commission received. Some accountants will retain the commission while others will operate on a fee basis and credit the commission against the time costs when rendering a bill — but do ask. The latter are more likely to provide impartial advice.

You should also enquire into the level of their advice. Some will link directly with the finance house while others will advise on the structure of the pension arrangement but link with a broker who will select the investment house. Again the latter approach is more likely to produce the best advice, unless the firm has sufficient 'in-house' expertise.

On balance, those who are able to offer sound impartial advice are more likely to come from some firms of accountants, actuaries, and independent pensions brokers.

Chapter 16
Administration of Personal Pension Schemes

The full extent of the administrative systems and requirements will not be known until all the detailed regulations have been absorbed, but a number of administrative matters need to be considered.

A PPS requires approval of the Board of Inland Revenue before the tax benefits can be received. Early approval may be granted from 1 August 1987 for a scheme to begin on 1 July 1988, although in practice there is likely to be a long waiting list. Provisional clearance may be granted by the regulations made by the Board in respect of applications made before 1 August 1989, providing the Board are satisfied that all the conditions of the scheme apply.

The Board will need to be satisfied that it adequately provides for the making, acceptance and application of transfer payments. As with Occupational schemes the Board may withdraw approval, but such approval cannot be backdated to a time earlier than the date when the relevant facts were such that they did not warrant the continuation of approval. Income tax under Schedule E may be payable on unauthorised payments from an approved PPS. Benefits provided by excess contributions may be taxed as unearned. (The difference between earned and unearned income could become more relevant again if the investment income surcharge is reintroduced.)

There are appeal procedures when the Board can refuse or withdraw approval. There are also provisions to exclude double relief and enable the Board to request information from scheme administrators. Any person who knowingly makes a false statement or representation shall be liable to a penalty not exceeding £500. Failure to furnish information can result in a penalty as set out in Section 98 TMA 1970.

Personal Pension Scheme Certificate

The Occupational Pensions Board will issue 'appropriate scheme certificates' to Personal pension schemes which satisfy the legal requirements for receiving 'minimum contributions' from the DHSS. The information required in respect of an appropriate scheme certificate is set out in Appendix 15. The DHSS Central Office at Newcastle upon Tyne will pay minimum contributions to an appropriate PPS when asked to do so on a standard form completed jointly by the individual concerned (ie the employee) and a representative of the PPS (ie the employer).

The DHSS will calculate what is due, including the 2 per cent incentive payment, from earnings information which employers have to send to the Inland Revenue after each tax year. They will send the minimum contributions to the PPS by way of Bankers Automated Clearing Services. If the individual wants the minimum contributions to stop or to go to another PPS if he changes job, he will have to tell the DHSS. Employers have to notify the DHSS when an employee ceases to be contracted out of SERPS. The information to be included in an application for an appropriate scheme certificate and the further information which may be required are set out in Appendices 15 and 16.

Incentive Payment for Occupational Schemes

The employer will claim the incentive payment for each of his eligible employees by entering the reference number of his Personal pension scheme on the end of year return he makes to the Inland Revenue. The DHSS will send the incentive payment to the scheme by way of Bankers Automated Clearing Services.

There are special provisions safeguarding members' protected rights where a PPS loses or surrenders its appropriate scheme certificate, and where a Money purchase scheme ceases to be contracted out.

Other Matters

The regulations also require schemes to:

— make available, on specified terms, information about the contribution and rules of the scheme;
— send to scheme members basic factual information about the scheme and members' rights under it (eg names of members, spouses and beneficiaries etc);
— provide information on the request of beneficiaries and spouses of members;
— provide information to members to enable them to remain informed about the performance of their scheme's investments, and the financial position of the provider and audited accounts of the scheme.

So as to monitor the total tax relief on a PPS it is proposed that the following procedures will apply:

(a) employees who join a PPS will have to provide the

scheme managers with a certificate from their employer before tax relief can be given at source. The certificate will attest that

— the individual is a genuine employee;
— he is not currently a member of an Occupational pension scheme to which the employer contributes;
— he is not, to the employer's knowledge, currently a member of another PPS, and
— no other certificate has been provided for that employee by other employers in the current tax year.

(b) the certificate will also provide information such as:

— the employee's national insurance number;
— the employee's current taxable salary;
— contributions payable by the employer.

The scheme manager can then check that the proposed contribution is within the permitted maximum.

(c) managers operating schemes to which the self-employed may also contribute need to distinguish between employees who will qualify for tax relief at source and the self-employed who will not.
(d) employees who wish to carry forward unused relief from previous years or carry back premiums to the preceding year will need to obtain certificates from their employers for each of the relevant years.

Appendix 1

Annuity Rates

June 1987 — Compulsory purchase

Payable monthly in advance, guaranteed for five years.

Age	Male		Female	
	Flat rate	5% escalation	Flat rate	5% escalation
Single person	£ per £000	£ per £000	£ per £000	£ per £000
70	12.30	9.47	11.08	8.17
65	11.20	8.26	10.20	7.18
60	10.37	7.32	9.57	6.45
55	9.73	6.59	9.13	5.92
50	9.24	6.03	8.84	5.53

Paid to member and widow/er

Member	spouse	Flat rate (M)	5% esc (M)	Flat rate (F)	5% esc (F)
70	65	9.65	6.68	9.79	6.88
65	65	9.44	6.45	9.44	6.45
65	60	9.13	6.05	9.23	6.19
60	60	8.99	5.89	8.99	5.89
60	55	8.79	5.60	8.85	5.70

Paid to member and 50 per cent to widow/er

Member	spouse	Flat rate (M)	5% esc (M)	Flat rate (F)	5% esc (F)
70	65	10.81	7.84	10.40	7.47
65	65	10.25	7.24	9.80	6.80
65	60	10.06	6.98	9.69	6.65
60	60	9.63	6.53	9.27	6.16
60	55	9.51	6.35	9.19	6.05

Note: The above rates are the pension per month per £1,000 of purchase money and are subject to a per policy deduction of £1.50. The rates also assume that the purchase monies are the proceeds of a maturing Standard Life pension contract.

Source: Standard Life

Appendix 2

Income Tax Rates 1987/88

Taxable income		Taxable income between	Rate	Cumulative Tax
	£	£	%	£
Basic-rate				
First	17,900	0–17,900	27	4,833
Higher-rates				
Next	2,500	17,901–20,400	40	5,833
	5,000	20,401–25,400	45	8,083
	7,900	25,401–33,300	50	12,033
	7,900	33,301–41,200	55	16,378
Above	41,200		60	

These rates will also apply where a wife's earnings election is made. An election may be of advantage if a married couple have a joint *gross* income in excess of £26,870, of which the wife's earnings are £6,545.

Appendix 3

Corporation Tax Rates 1987/88

	%
Year to 31 March 1988	
Profits above £500,000	35
Profits below £100,000	27
Profits of £100,000 to £500,000	
— on the first £100,000	27
— on the excess	37

The above bands are reduced by the number of associated companies.

Appendix 4

Tax Treatment of Usual Forms of Investment

Form of Investment	Form of tax (see note)
Pension scheme	Tax-free
Bank or building society deposits	IT
Property — income therefrom	IT
— gain on sale if private residence	Tax-free
if held as trading stock	IT
if held as investment	CGT
Local authority bonds	IT
Government stock — income therefrom	IT
— gain on sale	Tax-free
Unit trusts or stocks and shares	
— on income	IT
— gain on sale	CGT
Single premium bond	30% tax on profit in bond. Higher-rate IT on encashment
Endowment policy	30% tax on profit in bond. Proceeds tax-free if held for at least seven and a half years
Purchased life annuity — capital element	Tax-free
— income element	IT
National savings — income bonds	IT
— certificates (restriction on return and investment)	Tax-free

Note: IT = income tax at 27-60 per cent
       CGT = capital gains tax at 30 per cent

Appendix 5

Definition of Incapacity

Personal pension schemes and retirement annuity contracts

The individual is 'incapable through infirmity of body or mind of carrying on his own occupation or any occupation of a similar nature for which he is trained or fitted.'

Company schemes

The SFO defines it as 'Physical or mental deterioration which is bad enough to prevent the individual following his normal employment, or which seriously impairs his earning capacity'. It does not merely mean a reduction in energy or ability.

'Exceptional circumstances of ill health' applies where the expectation of life is unquestionably short by comparison with the average for the same age and sex.

Appendix 6

Early Retirement

Provision is available to allow the Inland Revenue discretion in approving benefits at an earlier age if it relates to an individual whose occupation is one in which 'persons customarily retire before attaining age 60' (section 226(3)(c) Income and Corporation Taxes Act 1970), and a list is given below of the occupations for which early ages have been agreed by the Inland Revenue at the time of writing.

Age 35   Athletes
Badminton players
Boxers
Cyclists
Dancers
Footballers (see note)
National Hunt jockeys
Rugby League players
Squash players
Table tennis players
Tennis players
Wrestlers

Age 40   Cricketers
Divers (saturation, deep-sea and free-swimming)
Golfers
Motorcycle riders; motorcross or road racing
Motor racing drivers
Speedway riders
Trapeze artistes

Age 45   Jockeys, flat-racing

Age 50   Croupiers
         Moneybroker dealers
         Newscasters
         Offshore riggers
         Royal Navy Reservists
         Rugby League referees
         Territorial Army Members

Age 55   Air pilots
         Brass instrumentalists
         Distant water trawlermen
         Firemen (part-time)
         Inshore fishermen
         Moneybroker dealer directors
         Nurses; physiotherapists; midwives or health visitors who are female
         National Health psychiatrists
         Singers

Note: Registered Football League players in England are covered by a pension scheme financed by the Football League and are therefore not eligible for a retirement annuity contract unless they have another source of earnings.

Appendix 7

National Insurance Contribution Rates 1987/88

Class 1 (Employee)

Level of earnings	Not contracted-out contribution rate on total	
	Employer %	Employee %
£39.00—£64.99 per week	5.00	5.00
£65.00—£99.99 per week	7.00	7.00
£100.00—£149.99 per week	9.00	9.00
£150.00—£295.00 per week	10.45	9.00
Over £295 per week	10.45	9.00 (on £295 only)

		Contracted-out contribution rates		
		Employer %		Employee %
£39.00—£64.99 per week	on £39	5.00	on £39	5.00
	on balance	0.90	on balance	2.85
£65.00—£99.99 per week	on £39	7.00	on £39	7.00
	on balance	2.90	on balance	4.85
£100.00—£149.99 per week	on £39	9.00	on £39	9.00
	on balance	4.90	on balance	6.85
£150.00—£295.00 per week	on £39	10.45	on £39	9.00
	on balance	6.35	on balance	6.85
over £295.00 per week	on £39 and above £295	10.45	on £39	9.00
	plus between £39 and £295	6.35	on £39 to £295	6.85
			above £295	nil

Class 2 (Self-employed) £3.85 per week
(if earnings exceed £2,125 per annum)

Class 3 (Voluntary) £3.75 per week

Class 4 (Self-employed earnings related) 6.3 per cent on profits between £4,590 and £15,340 per annum. Income tax relief on one-half of the contributions.

Appendix 8

Social Security Benefits 1987/88

	Weekly £	Annual £
Retirement pension — single	39.50	2,054
— couple	63.25	3,289
Age addition (over 80)	0.25	13

Reduced under the 'earnings rule' where a man under 70 or a woman under 65 earns more than £75 per week.

Widow's pension
Maximum if widowed at 50 or over reduced by 7 per cent for each year below 50; ineligible below 40. £39.50 £2,054

Widow's allowance (tax-free) £55.35 (for 26 weeks only)

Widowed mother's allowance £39.50 £2,054

Child dependant addition (tax-free) £8.05 £419

Child Benefit is payable (tax-free) to a mother at the rate of £7.25 per week for each child under 16 (up to 19 if at school) plus £4.70 for first eligible child of single parent family.

National Insurance contracting-out rebates

	1987/88		Proposed 1988/89	
	Net of tax rate	Employee's rate grossed-up at 27 per cent	Net of tax rate	Employee's rate grossed-up at 27 per cent
	%	%	%	%
Employer	4.10	4.10	3.80	3.80
Employee	2.15	2.95	2.00	2.74
	6.25	7.05	5.80	6.54
Incentive payment	2.00	2.00	2.00	2.00
	8.25	9.05	7.80	8.54

Appendix 9

Pension Definitions

20 per cent Director

Means a director who, either alone or together with his/her spouse and minor children, is or becomes the beneficial owner of shares which when added to any shares held by the trustees of any settlement to which the director or his/her spouse has transferred assets, carry more than 20 per cent of the voting rights in the company providing the pension or in a company which controls that company.

5 per cent Director or controlling director

Means a controlling director as defined in section 224(1) Income and Corporation Taxes Act 1970, ie, a director of a company, the directors of which have a controlling interest and who is the beneficial owner of, or able either directly or indirectly to control more than 5 per cent of the ordinary share capital of the company.

20 per cent and Controlling directors

The special provisions which apply to 20 per cent directors (including an employee who was a controlling director within the last 10 years) are as follows:

(a) averaging is always required in the calculation of final remuneration, save only on the calculation of death benefits;

(b) in calculating maximum entitlement to pension, retirement annuity benefits must be taken into account to ensure that total benefits do not exceed 2/3 final remuneration, even where the benefits provided under the scheme do not exceed straight sixtieths. A similar restriction applies to the calculation of the maximum entitlement to tax-free cash. This provision also applies to a 5 per cent director or controlling director;

(c) on death in service on or after 75th birthday, discretionary disposal will normally not apply to the death benefits provided;

(d) if all benefits are deferred beyond normal retirement date, maximum benefits will generally be calculated on the basis that the date on which benefits are taken is treated as normal retirement date. Where cash is taken and pension deferred, the date of taking cash is treated as normal retirement date and the pension is calculated also at that date but may subsequently be increased by reference to the Retail Price Index.

These restrictions apply for deferment up to age 70, but the normal provisions apply to periods of deferment beyond age 70;

(e) a woman cannot take early benefits at 55 but must wait until age 60.

The restrictions which apply to 5 per cent directors or controlling directors are less stringent unless of course the controlling director is also a 20 per cent director. Otherwise the controlling director may have benefits on the basis applying to ordinary employees.

Appendix 10

Pension Benefits

	Maximum pension at normal retirement date expressed as percentage of final salary.	
Years of service to normal retirement date	*Employees and directors joining a scheme*	
	(i) before 17 March 1987	*(ii) after 16 March 1987*
1	1.67	3.33
2	3.33	6.67
3	5.00	10.00
4	6.67	13.33
5	8.33	16.67
6	13.33	20.00
7	26.67	23.33
8	40.00	26.67
9	53.33	30.00
10	66.67	33.33
11	66.67	36.67
12	66.67	40.00
13	66.67	43.33
14	66.67	46.67
15	66.67	50.00
16	66.67	53.33
17	66.67	56.67
18	66.67	60.00
19	66.67	63.33
20	66.67	66.67

Appendix 11

Inland Revenue Limits — Transitional Rules

The Chancellor's broad intention is that employees who were in service and members of a scheme before 17 March 1987 and who remain with the same employer or who effectively remain members of the same scheme should not be adversely affected by the changes. It is difficult to lay down clear guidelines which will apply in every case: in some cases it may be necessary to consider the relevant facts before determining whether a scheme (or member) is 'new'. In general, the following situations will *not* normally be regarded as caught by the changes:

   (i) restructuring of a business resulting in employees moving from one employer's scheme to another's, *provided that* both employers are within the same group;
   (ii) a move on promotion from one scheme of an employer to another scheme of that same employer;
   (iii) a move to a new or existing scheme of a new employer who has taken over the old employer (or his business), *provided that* the individual was a member of the old employer's scheme;
   (iv) changes in the benefit structure of an existing scheme, *provided that* such changes do not give accelerated rates of accrual under the pre-17 March 1987 rules where these were not previously available;
   (v) the exercise of a power of augmentation under the rules of an existing scheme to improve the benefits available to a member who joined before 17 March 1987;
   (vi) schemes or arrangements in existence established before 17 March 1987, even if by then all the relevant

documentation had not been finalised or no application for tax approval had been made. This will usually depend on the facts of a particular case but, as a general rule, a scheme will be considered as existing if the employer has entered into a contractual obligation before 17 March to provide benefits;

(vii) individuals who cease to be members of their employer's scheme (whether or not they leave the employer's service), *provided that* they rejoin the scheme within one month;

(viii) employees serving a waiting period before becoming full members of the employer's scheme, *provided that* they were members in respect of some benefits at least (eg Death-in-service benefits) before 17 March 1987.

Appendix 12

Illustrated Funding of Pension Scheme — Workings

Age	Salary escalating at 5 per cent £	Contribution rate at 16 per cent per annum £	Accumulated fund growing at 10 per cent per annum £
45	30,000	4,800	5,280
46	31,500	5,040	11,352
47	33,075	5,292	18,308
48	34,729	5,557	26,252
49	36,465	5,834	35,295
50	38,288	6,126	45,563
51	40,203	6,432	57,195
52	42,213	6,754	70,344
53	44,324	7,092	85,179
54	46,540	7,446	101,888
55	48,867	7,819	120,677
56	51,310	8,210	141,776
57	53,876	8,620	165,435
58	56,569	9,051	191,935
59	59,398	9,504	221,583
60	62,368	9,979	254,718
61	65,486	10,478	291,715
62	68,760	11,002	332,988
63	72,199	11,552	378,994
64	75,808	12,129	430,236

Appendix 13

Net Relevant Earnings

Relevant earnings

This means:

1. Emoluments chargeable under Schedule E from an office or employment held by the individual.
2. Income from any property which is attached to or forms part of the emoluments of an office or employment held by him.
3. Income which is chargeable under Schedule D arising from his trade, profession or vocation (either as an individual or as a partner acting personally in a partnership).
4. Income treated as earned income by virtue of section 383 ICTA 1970 (patent royalties).

The following income is excluded:

(a) emoluments of a director of a company whose income derives wholly or mainly from investment income if the individual, either alone or together with any other persons who are or have been at any time directors of the company, controls the company;
(b) earnings from an office which is already in a pension scheme;
(c) anything in respect of which tax is chargeable under Schedule E and which arises from the acquisition or disposal of shares or an interest in shares or from a right to acquire shares (ie share option gains and share incentive income

which is taxable under section 186 ICTA 1970 or section 79(4) or (7) Finance Act 1972 or section 38(5) Finance Act 1984. Also gains from the sale of profit sharing scheme shares under section 55(1) Finance Act 1978);
(d) termination payments under section 187 ICTA 1970, including golden handshakes.

The following deductions must be made from the above 'relevant earnings' to produce 'net relevant earnings' upon which the maximum levels of pension contributions are based:

1. Annuities, royalties and rents etc which are to be deducted from earnings under section 130(l), (n) or (o) ICTA 1970.
2. Expenses under sections 189, 192 or 194(3) ICTA 1970.
3. Stock relief under Schedule 9 or 10 Finance Act 1981.
4. Losses or capital allowances arising from activities, profits or gains of the individual, which would be included in computing relevant earnings of the individual's wife or husband.

The employee's share of minimum contributions paid by the DHSS shall be ignored so as not to reduce the scope for pension planning.

Appendix 14

Dependant's Pension

The Personal pension scheme may (and in certain circumstances must) be structured so that it provides for a pension to the widow, widower or dependant of the member after his or her death. Therefore it could be payable to the member's children. The pension can be up to 100 per cent of the member's pension. Therefore the same level of pension could continue to be paid to the surviving spouse after the death of the member. The pension may be deferred until the surviving spouse reaches the age of 60 and be paid from that date if preferred.

The pension may cease before the death of the dependant if:

1. He or she marries, or
2. If the spouse is under 45 and has no dependants under the age of 18 when she reaches the age of 45.
3. It is paid to a person under 18 and is structured to cease when he becomes 18 or ceases full-time education (unless he was a dependant of the member otherwise than by reason only that he was under 18).
4. The pension may be for a set term of under 10 years which may expire upon the marriage of the annuitant, his attaining the age of 18 or if later ceasing to be in full-time education.

If no pension as described above is paid, then on the death of the member a lump sum representing no more than the return of contributions together with reasonable interest on contributions or bonuses out of profit may be paid to the estate.

Appendix 15

Information for an Appropriate Scheme Certificate

1. Every application for an appropriate scheme certificate shall be made in writing and shall include the following particulars:

(a) the name of the scheme and the address where it is administered;
(b) the names and addresses of the trustees (if any) and administrators of the scheme;
(c) the name, address and standing (in relation to the scheme) of the person applying for the certificate, if he is not the trustees or administrators, or one or some of them;
(d) the name and address of the person who or body which has established or proposed to establish the scheme;
(e) the nature of the scheme;
(f) the name and address of a bank which accepts payments made by automated direct credit transfer and the name and number of the account at the bank, into which it is desired that minimum contributions should be paid; and
(g) the date from which it is desired that the certificate shall have effect;
(h) such evidence as the Board may reasonably require that the scheme satisfies such of the requirements of the relevant regulations as apply to it.

2. Every application shall be accompanied by a copy of:

(a) the documents constituting the scheme; and
(b) the rules of the scheme, if they are not set out in those documents or any of them,

except where the Board in their discretion dispense wholly or partly with this requirement.

3. Every person who makes an application shall supply such other documents and information as the Board may reasonably require.

The appropriate scheme certificate shall specify the name of the scheme and the address where it is administered and the date from which the certificate is to have effect.

Appendix 16

Further Information on Change of Circumstances

A person to whom an appropriate scheme certificate has been issued shall, in such manner and at such times as the Board may reasonably require, furnish to the Board such reports, accounts and other documents and information relating to the scheme to which the certificate relates as the Board may reasonably require, and, in particular, shall notify the Board of:

(a) any change in the identity, names or addresses of the trustees (if any) and administrators of the scheme;
(b) any change in the name or address of the person who or body which has established the scheme;
(c) any change in the nature of the scheme; and
(d) any such change of circumstances affecting the scheme as the Board may have required him to notify,

as soon as practicable after its occurrence.

Aberdeen · Birmingham · Bristol · Glasgow · Leeds · London · Manchester · Norwich · Nottingham · Sunderland

WHERE TO OBTAIN FURTHER INFORMATION

IF YOU NEED ADVICE ON ANY OF THE FOLLOWING MATTERS, COMPLETE AND RETURN THIS FORM OR A PHOTOCOPY TO THE AUTHOR, BARRY STILLERMAN, AT THE ADDRESS BELOW.

Please Tick

☐ EMPLOYERS CONTRACTING OUT

☐ THE NEW AVC ARRANGEMENTS

☐ IMPROVING PENSION BENEFITS

☐ SETTING UP OR MODIFYING A COMPANY SCHEME

☐ THE NEW PERSONAL PENSION SCHEME

☐ EXECUTIVE SCHEMES

☐ ANY OTHER MATTERS

NAME _____

COMPANY _____

POSITION _____

ADDRESS _____

_____

_____

TELEPHONE NUMBER _____

COMPLETE AND RETURN THE COUPON TO: BARRY STILLERMAN FCA, PARTNER, STOY HAYWARD, 8 BAKER STREET, LONDON W1M 1DA. TELEPHONE 01-486 5888

Stoy Hayward
A Member of Horwath & Horwath International
ACCOUNTANTS · BUSINESS ADVISERS · MANAGEMENT CONSULTANTS

STOY HAYWARD, 8 BAKER STREET, LONDON W1M 1DA TELEPHONE 01-486 5888

Index

Additional Voluntary
   Contributions (AVC) 41, 48,
   68, 92, 101-7, 120, 150
   free-standing 68, 104, 106-7
   one-off 105
   Tax benefits 103
Advice on investment 177-81
   Financial Services Act 1986
     177-8, 180
Age pension payable 9, 13, 16,
   19-20, 53-8, 61, 140
Annuity rates 16, 187

Banks 9, 174
   advice from 178, 179
   tax on investments 190
Brokers
   advice from 178, 179-80, 181
   commission 172-4, 177
   independent intermediaries
     172, 179-80
   investment performance 163-72
   personal pension schemes 173
Building Societies 9, 174

Cash
   pension commuted in special
     case 57
   tax-free *see* Tax-free cash
Chartered accountants 180-1
Child
   death-in-service benefit 35
   pension for 80, 119
   social security benefits 196
Company pension scheme 8,
   66-71, 85, 141
   Additional Voluntary
     Contributions 101-7
   choice of 66-7, 70-1
   early retirement 53-7
   employee's incapacity 191
   employee's payment into 9
   final salary scheme 20, 55, 57
   group 174
   managed schemes 164-7
   opting out 10, 141-3
   pension-linked mortgage 48-9
   self-administered 94-5
   tax-free lump-sums 37-8
   'top hat' scheme 67, 96-8, 113
   topping up 28, 105, 107, 120
   'uplifted eightieths' scale' 38
Consulting actuary 180

Death-in-service 34-6, 92, 97,
   121-4, 131, 149, 151, 198, 199
   life assurance 121-4, 151
   personal pension scheme 149,
     151
   salary sacrifice 125
Deferred pension 53, 57-8, 130-2,
   133, 151, 199, 206
Dependants 80, 119, 151, 206
   death-in-service benefits 35,
     80, 149, 151
   personal pension scheme
     149, 151
Director 66, 87, 198-9
   dividend payments 61
   national insurance 59-61
   net relevant earnings 204
   occupational pension 85
   pension-linked mortgage 49
   personal pension scheme 78
   purchase of premises 50-1
   self-administered scheme 94-5
   tax-free cash 39-40
   'top hat' scheme 67, 96-8, 113
   topping-up 105, 107
Doctors and dentists 159-61

Employee 13-14, 31, 66-7, 78
   Additional Voluntary
     Contributions 68, 101-7
   Death-in-service benefits 34-6,
     92, 97, 121-4

incapacity 57, 191
job mobility 9, 11, 44, 49, 66,
  68-9, 87, 93, 104, 129-37,
  140, 151, 179
national insurance 59-61,
  75-6, 194
occupational pension 85
'one-off' payment into
  Company scheme 9
opting out of company scheme
  10, 141
pension-linked mortgage 48
personal pension scheme 67,
  69-70, 78, 85, 139, 141-6,
  185-6
pre March 1987 scheme 201-2
previously controlling director
  198
tax-free lump-sums 37-8
Employer 14
contributions to personal
  pension scheme 85, 142-3,
  185
guidelines for 65-71
national insurance 60, 75-6, 194
occupational pension 85, 127
State Earnings Related Pension
  Scheme 60, 65, 184
Executive 'top hat' scheme 67,
  96-8, 113

Final remuneration
  artificial inflation 112-13
  dynamisation 113, 114-15
  salary sacrifice 125
Final salary scheme 20, 55, 57, 65,
  67, 70, 87-91
  contracting out 80-3
  funding 116-7, 126-7
  job mobility 131-2, 133
  new simplified arrangements
    98-9
Flat-rate pension 25, 27-8,
  117-18
Friendly societies 174

Group scheme 66, 82, 129, 137,
  174
Guaranteed Minimum Pension
  (GMP) 74
  job mobility 131-2, 134-5

Hybrid scheme 67, 96

Incapacity 57, 191
Industry-wide scheme 93-4
Inflation 16, 24-5, 117-18
  escalating pension 117-18
  inflation-proof pension 25
  rising pension 25

Job mobility 9, 11, 44, 49, 66,
  68-9, 87, 129-37, 140, 179
  Additional Voluntary
    Contributions 104, 106
  industry-wide scheme 93-4
  personal pension scheme 151

Life assurance
  based investments 12
  pension scheme 121-4, 151
  self-employed 158-9
Loan-backs 98-9
Lump-sum payment *see* Tax-free
  cash

Money purchase scheme 21, 58,
  65, 66, 67, 86-7, 88-91, 117
  Additional Voluntary
    Contributions 101-2
  contracted-out (COMPS) 80,
    82, 136, 185
  funding 115-17
  job mobility 132, 134, 136
  new simplified arrangements
    67, 91-3, 102, 109-10
  pension level 109-10, 115-17
  topping-up 117
Mortgages
  endowment-linked 44-5
  pension-linked 45-52, 106, 150
  personal pension scheme 150
  repayment 44

National insurance
  contributions (NICs) 59-61,
    61-2, 73
  contracting out of state pension
    scheme 75-6, 197
  rates 194-5
  salary sacrifice 125
  self-employed 60, 195
  voluntary 60, 195
Net relevant earnings (NRE)
  144-5, 155-6, 204
New simplified arrangements 67,
  91-3
  final salary scheme 92-3

Index

money purchase scheme 91-3, 102
   restrictions 93

Occupational pension scheme 67, 73, 85-99
   Additional Voluntary Contributions 101-7
   death-in-service 151
   final salary scheme 87-91
   incentive payment 185
   industry-wide scheme 93-4
   Inland Revenue approval 183
   leaving scheme but not job 133
   life assurance 121
   loan backs 98-9
   maximum levels 109, 110, 115
   money purchase schemes 86-7
   open-market option 175
   self-administered scheme 94-5
   topping-up 105, 107, 120
   transfers from and to personal pension scheme 136-7
   see also Company pension scheme
Open-market option 175, 179
Over-funding 126-7
Overseas income 161

Partners *see* Self-employed
Pension 15-19, 81, 163
   benefits 200
   early payment 53-7
   flat-rate 16
Pension fund
   investment performance 163-75, 179
   management 70-1, 164-7
   sector selection 167-9
   unit-linked 169-70
   with-profit 170-1
Pension providers 152
Personal pension scheme (PPS) 8, 10, 38, 49, 67, 69-70, 85, 133, 139-52, 161
   administration 183-6
   administrative charges 173
   age payable 9, 20, 53-7, 140, 154
   aims 139-40
   benefits 148-51
   certificate 184, 185, 207-9
   death-in-service 149, 151
   DHSS contributions 144, 148, 184, 205
   employers' contributions 85, 142-3, 144-5
   excess contributions 183
   incapacity 191
   incentive payments 78-9, 185
   Inland Revenue approval 183-4
   job mobility 135-7, 140, 151
   managed schemes 164-7
   maximum contributions 143-5, 151
   minimum contributions 148
   money purchase basis 140, 149
   open-market option 175
   pension level 109-10, 117
   pension providers 152
   problems 140-3
   protected rights 148, 175, 185
   roll-up fund 148, 151
   self-employed 153-6
   starting date 139
   tax benefits 145-8, 183, 185, 186
   tax-free cash 40, 149, 150, 156, 158
   topping-up 105, 120
   transfers from and to occupational pension scheme 136-7
   widow, widower or dependent 119, 149, 206
   year of assessment 145-8, 186
Property
   inheritance tax 52
   purchase 50-2 *see also* Mortgage
   trading down 26-7

Reforming Social Security 8
Retirement 9, 13, 16, 19-20, 53-8, 61, 140, 192-3
   incapacity causing 57, 191
   post-retirement costs 25
Retirement annuity (RAP) 153-5
   incapacity 191
   maximum limits 155-6
   pension level 109-10, 117
   tax-free cash 156, 158
   topping-up 105, 120, 143
   waiver of premiums 162
   window or widower's pension 119-20
Rising pension 25
Roll-up fund 29, 32-3, 53, 57
   personal pension scheme 148, 151

The Daily Telegraph Pensions Guide

Salary sacrifice 106, 124-5
Section 32 Buy-out policy 130, 134-5
Self-administered scheme 67, 94-5
  charges 174
  hybrid 96
  loan-backs 98-9
  tax 95
Self-employed 13-14, 31, 78, 153-62
  life assurance 158-9
  national insurance contributions 60, 195
  pension-linked mortgage 48, 49
  personal pension scheme 139, 153-6, 186
  retirement annuity scheme 153-5
  self-managed schemes 162
  tax-free cash 10, 38, 48
  topping up 105
Self-managed scheme 162
Share option or incentive schemes 112
Social security benefits 196-7
Sole traders *see* Self-employed
Solicitors 180, 181
Spouse 15, 16, 80
  death-in-service benefits 34-6, 92, 97, 121-4
State Earnings Related Pension Scheme (SERPS) 61-3, 73, 74-5
  changes to 73
  contracting out 60, 65-6, 73-83, 140-3, 175, 184
  widow 62
State pension 27, 59-63, 66, 74-5, 196
  basic 61
  contracting out 60, 73-83, 140-3, 179, 197
  national insurance 59-61

Tax 16, 190
  Additional Voluntary Contributions 103
  annual pension 16
  benefits 13, 29-36, 30-1, 66, 171-2
  capital gains 32
  carrying forward or back 145-8, 186
  corporation 50, 127, 189
  deferral 33-4
  income 188
  inheritance 34-6, 52, 58, 151, 159
  on investments 190
  life assurance 158-9
  loan-backs 99
  maximum pension limit 22, 53
  national insurance 60
  overseas income 161
  personal pension scheme 145-8, 183, 185, 186
  relief 9, 12-13, 79
  roll-up 29, 32-3, 53
  widow's pension 80, 119
Tax-free cash 15-16, 16, 29, 37-52, 53, 131
  abuse 39-40, 113
  Additional Voluntary Contributions 105-6
  deferred pension 57
  effect on annual pension 37
  limit 8-9, 40-3, 48
  pension-linked mortgage 45-52
  personal pension scheme 149, 150, 156, 158
  retirement annuity (RAP) 156, 158
'Top hat' scheme 67, 96-8, 113
Topping-up 105, 117, 120
Transferring between schemes 8, 130-4

Widow 118-21, 124, 131, 149, 187, 196, 206
  benefits 92, 97, 196
  contracted out schemes 74, 80
  pension 80
  State Earnings Related Pension 62
Widower's pension 80, 119, 149, 151, 187, 206